Daily
Affirmations
For *Love*

365 days of LOVE in though
and action

Daily Affirmations For *Love*

365 days of LOVE in thought and action

Mamiko Odegard, Ph.D.

Biz Life Success Publishing, LLC

Scottsdale, Arizona

Published by:

Biz Life Success Publishing, LLC

Scottsdale, Arizona

ISBN : 0615679056; 978-0615679051

Printed in the United States of America

Copyright ©2016

10 9 8 7 6 5 4 3

Mamiko Odegard, PhD

9375 E Shea Blvd, Suite 100

Scottsdale, Arizona 85260

CONTACT:

(480) 391-1184

www.dailyaffirmationsforlove.com/

http://www.drmamiko.com/

Success@DrMamiko.com

Praise for Daily Affirmations For Love

Every moment, small gesture, and awareness becomes a gift. Dr. Odegard designed a collection of daily thoughts to reflect upon and open our hearts throughout the year. She has captured a slice of humanity with her thoughtful and loving approach to each day. Dr. Odegard clearly has a keen eye for the simple pleasures in life. Each page is filled with gentle, funny—and at times - profound insights. This is a must read for every person who is passionate about their personal journey into relationships. Dr. Odegard challenges us to stop... reflect... and smile... as we live each day to the fullest. This little book will bring joy to your heart and those you love.

~ Jessica Browne, Actress
| Murder She Wrote

Beautiful! I like it.

The daily readings...

It's very personal...

It's passionate...

It stimulates good thoughts and actions...

I ran right in to give my wife a warm embrace and a "come and get me" kiss! I like how you repeat the themes through the year. DECEMBER 1st—Purpose, which in my way of thinking, drives everything. Of course I like your acknowledgement of God's blessing and guidance in your life. For me He is the essential in purpose and the power of love to transform. He is the author of marriage and all the "magic" you and Greg have discovered in your life together. You and Greg do have a unique relationship of focus, care, support, energy and passion. Many can read and be inspired. Congratulations on yet another achievement.

Best wishes for the success of Daily Affirmations for Love!

~ Edward G. Masters, Executive Consultant
| MAP

Dr. Odegard has captured the essence of a truly loving and committed relationship in her daily book of gentle reminders. As I read through each day, I am reminded of what's really important in life and love. She touches about every emotion I have by writing about the many facets of a love relationship. After reading it, I never realized how rewarded, fulfilled, and deep two people can be in relationship. And sometimes how much work is involved in a relationship. This book is a beautiful expression of gratitude for another being in someone's life. I've learned a lot from it. Filled with gratitude,

~**Lisa Jane Vargas**, Lead Clinical Outreach Coordinator | Sierra Tucson

Touching to the core of my consciousness – that is the level of personal empowerment Dr. Odegard's Daily Affirmations For Love brought to me. Thinking I would find the way to build romance into my relationships, I found instead a pathway to interacting with more love, honor, commitment and respect with anyone who matters to me. The surprise at the end of this book is who you become in the process of reading it! Embrace that it is little actions, consistently engaged on a daily basis, which can transform any relationship. The lessons learned allow us to consciously choose actions that will leave our love marked indelibly on the lives of every person with whom we connect.

~**Anna Weber,** Entrepreneur's Strategist
4-Dimensional Success

Although this book is about current relationships, I reflect on the memories of my late husband—my soul mate. All the thoughts, gestures, warm fuzzies, commitment, and activities we shared are reflected in your book. Having my personal thoughts written in the margin, as the years go by, these notes will become priceless. Each key word on the pages will be etched in my mind reminding me how precious a relationship can be if you "reach out and touch someone". 1 John 3:18 "My little children, let us not love in word or in tongue, but in deed and in truth."

~ **Francine Masterson**, Grief Recovery Specialist

Imagine having the relationship of your dreams and then being able to maintain the deep love and connection you felt when you first met... Are you excited to read this book yet? Because as you read through the pages, you will find it is about letting go of tired, worn out ideas that have kept you stuck and bringing in new ideas to awaken your best. It is about empowering yourself and your partner to create happiness, harmony and a holy union between you. It is about taking daily small steps that will lead to a whole new way of engaging each other, and in the process – finding out that you have changed and achieved the relationship you've always wanted.

~ Ken D. Foster, Founder | PremierCoaching.com

Dr. Odegard is magical in her writing. To have gone so far, and provided so much, in such a short book takes magic as well as discipline. In this book you will find simple heartfelt insights into aging, remorse, redemption, renewal, giving, receiving love, and the succession of love from one state into another. Mamiko shows us that love doesn't need to age as we do. Now that is astonishing! However, it is rare to see people keep love together as they age; that is what makes this book so special, and needed. She takes advantage of one ordinary moment after another and building the magic of love from it.

~ **Bruce Piasecki**, President and Founder | ACH Group

Dedication

Dearest Greg,

You are absolutely the love of my life! This book is an open proclamation of my love and gratitude as a tribute to you for the many ways you express affection for me. The words that follow throughout this book reflect how much you mean to me. I very much want to continue to love, honor, and appreciate you.

You have been the catalyst for my emergence as a happy, confident, and self-assured woman. Over the years, you gently and steadfastly believed in me and encouraged me in my career and all aspects of my life.

You also bring me more joy, love, and peace than I ever thought was possible. You express love openly and freely in so many ways. Emotionally and physically you are my biggest advocate. You are an excellent listener. You offer words of support by demonstrating unconditional love and acceptance. Your gentle, humorous, lighthearted, nurturing and affectionate ways give me permission to be myself. Your daily acts of love through kindness and consideration touch my heart and sped the passage of our many years together.

I am eternally grateful to you, Greg, for being such an incredible husband, lover, friend and confidant. You also lovingly demonstrate what a devoted and natural father you are to our daughter, Mariesa.

You possess an uncanny ability to help me feel special—as the most important person in your life. Your trust, your hugs, your passion, your love, and your belief in me lead to the best possible version of myself. You've taught me what intimacy is. May our love continue to grow year after year along with continued magic and fun.

I also appreciate your assistance with this book as my Editor-in-Chief. The birth of our daughter completed our circle of love making us a family. This book finds you and Mariesa typing and organizing the format. We wept tears when moved by passages within. I feel blessed far beyond my wildest dreams.

Thank you, my love. I am eternally grateful to be your chosen one, your wife.

All my love forever,

Mamiko

Table of Contents

About the Author

Dr. Mamiko Odegard is an international best-selling author and a highly acclaimed life and business coach who embraces her clients and audiences with passion and heart. She is the leading authority on overcoming self-sabotage, attaining maximum love and healthy relationships, and achieving world class performance Mamiko found her love and soul mate in Greg Odegard; it was practically love at first sight. To this day, after 40 years of marriage, Mamiko still adores and is in awe of Greg's many ways of demonstrating daily statements and actions which speak clearly of love. Thus, this book was borne to commemorate that a true and lasting love can be as fresh, lively, and passionate as the early years together. Their unique and loving relationship attracted nationwide attention, particularly the Dr. Laura Berman Show (Oprah Productions).

Mamiko speaks from experience as she shares the benefit of her experiences and personal growth—from one of shame to confidence and self-esteem, and ultimately learning to love and accept herself.

Mamiko's innovative coaching, encompasses over 30 years as a psychologist, individual and couples therapist, and seminar leader. She is also a sought out speaker, helping turn past wounds to EXTRAordinary self-love and acceptance. She is the creator of Conscious Loving™ and the YOU3 Program™, in which she helps individuals and couples transform to their best selves in mere days and weeks! She wants all to feel *Irresistible, Invincible, and Iconic*™ to leave a legacy of love.

Mamiko's genuine concern and care for all who cross her path is readily apparent. Her lifelong passion is helping individuals feel the happiness and peace from loving themselves, in order to experience success in all aspects of life and work. Each person deserves to feel cherished and be treated as the most important person in the world. Yes, we all deserve these!

Foreword

Robert Allen:

Mamiko's purpose in life is to help others fully experience the love and exuberance in loving and being loved by another. We all dream of having the type of love that is sustaining, fun, passionate, novel, yet familiar and supportive. Mamiko provides us an easy formula...consciously being open and taking small steps each day through affirmations.

Yes, we are all familiar with affirmations. We have come to associate these with the power of positive thinking. Mamiko takes a different approach. Hers is more than merely thinking that our love will become richer. She gently encourages us to continually view our partner in tender loving ways and to demonstrate daily multiple acts of love to our beloved. It is in carrying out these actions that the true essence of our love toward another is fully communicated and expressed. Our partner knows and can absolutely feel the adoration that emanates from genuine love.

The miracle is not in meeting Mr. or Ms. Right...It is the moment by moment gestures, comments, and ways of perceiving that special someone which contribute to the longevity of passion, commitment, and partnership. When we find our deepest lover, we find ourselves being emotionally, physically, and spiritually intimate. We can talk about our hopes, disappointments, frustrations, irritations, excitement, happiness, and fulfillment. No topic is off limits. We know the other fully and completely.

Mamiko provides real tools for all of us to manage our emotions and to talk and be supported by the ones who mean the most to us. Her wisdom for creating happiness, harmony, fun, and excitement allows all of us to feel our emotions and recapture those times when we felt so silly and totally in the moment. Too often we get caught up in being too serious, busy, and falling into mundane routines. This is why, Mamiko is like a breath of fresh air, allowing ordinary times to be savored and remembered.

She has a way of writing that is easily understandable and sometimes makes you want to smile or to be moved to tears...that a relationship has the possibility to be so close and beautiful. In the process of going through thoughts and acts of love, we notice we like ourselves more, accept ourselves and others, as we begin to deliberately view and treat ourselves and our mates with deep love, respect, and honor. Yes, cherishing does begin within each of us.

Congratulations! You are destisned to have the love you deserve.

~ Robert G. Allen, New York Times Best Selling Author, financial writer, real estate investor and motivational speaker. Allen is the author of several personal finance books and recently released a new book, which he co-authored with Mark Victor Hansen titled Cash in a Flash:Fast Money in Slow Times. It is the sequel to The One Minute Millionaire: The Enlightened Way to Wealth.

Acknowledgements

Many people over the years have contributed to the love, passion, and ideas presented in this book. The completion of this book took place due to labors of love and acts of kindness emanating from these significant persons in my life. My deepest gratitude and thanks to:

Our daughter, **Mariesa**, has taught me many lessons in love and patience, and has shown the undeniable gift of love between a mother and daughter and how beautiful a family relationship can be.

My parents, **Michiko and Enrique Martinez**, nurtured my growth and contributed to the person I am today.

Greg's parents, **Christine and Jerry Odegard**, gave the gift of a son who has made my daily life a miracle of love and blessings.

Rhonda Zaccone steadfastly believed in me and provided emotional and technical support throughout the publication process.

Francine Masterson helped me grow spiritually through her giving nature and through her prayers for our family and me.

Martina Martin inspired me to further explain some of my ideas so you, the reader, could more readily understand concepts and steps for building more loving relationships.

My **friends and countless valued clients**...who over the years touched me with their warmth, trust, and wisdom, and taught me that respect and love extends to all people that we meet as they contribute to our lessons of life.

Finally, my profound and genuine appreciation to **the pioneers in the field of counseling and optimal wellness** who influenced my professional and personal skills, and growth through their dynamic concepts and techniques. **Carl Rogers** formulated the art of reflective listening to show understanding and empathy. **Sharon Wegscheider-Cruse** focused on healing the 'inner child" to grow into a healthier, more fulfilled adult; and

Albert Ellis emphasized the importance of recognizing and changing erroneous thinking. Centuries old Buddhist practices such as mindfulness merging with modern approaches serve to foster more acceptance in oneself and others. More contemporary therapists, such as Barbara DeAngeles and John Gray defined the "love letter" approach to encouraging and writing about one's feelings which affect a relationship; Harville Hendrix and Helen Hunt refined techniques in listening and responding to another; and Gary Chapman delineated and raised the awareness of the five ways we can express love.

Introduction

This book was inspired and written to express love and gratitude to my husband, Greg. As our anniversary approached, I wanted to give him a very personal present. I felt the ultimate gift would be a book expressing my many sentiments about him. I not only wanted to acknowledge and celebrate our relationship, but to thank Greg for being such a spontaneously loving person. He has brought me complete happiness and affection—more than I ever imagined was possible. This is my way of openly proclaiming my love to my sweetheart... the man of my dreams.

Daily Affirmations for Love can be used daily to recognize, remember, and celebrate the love and warmth toward a special someone in your life. It is my hope that this book can be read as a couple or individually to grow in one's awareness of how to truly love oneself and to show that same type of tenderness and love towards others. These expressions of love through verbal communication and acts of kindness can be shared with lovers, parents, children, and friends.

Dear readers, I hope that you can all experience the closeness, romance, passion, joys, peace, and dreams that are possible in all relationships. Although you will find yearlong meditations for each day, you may begin anytime or anywhere in the book. It is not a workbook but rather a collection of daily affirmations to promote love. It can be used to increase the awareness of the gifts and possibilities open to you in every loving relationship. Whether you read it as a couple or individually, have fun doing the suggested activity for the day. Many of the activities can be modified to do with a partner or they can be done alone. Simply open to any page and begin. There are ideas for small and large actions, and changes in perspective that you can use daily to show your love. Thoughtful gestures and words can quickly and powerfully enhance a relationship.

Sometimes, you might have difficulty knowing what healthy love is. This book provides a blueprint for recognizing and showing true love in unending ways. A number of affirmations detail looking inward within yourself. It is to emphasize the importance of starting with yourself first. When you desire improvements in your relationships, you typically expect the other to change, thinking that your life would be instantly transformed for the better. Unfortunately, this thinking is flawed, as it encourages us to be manipulative, both subtly and outwardly—resulting in anger, resentment, and even more resistance to change by your loved ones. By cherishing yourself and extending your affection to another, you increase the chances of attracting, developing, and keeping the loving relationship that you've always wanted.

This book encompasses more than the lessons learned throughout our remarkable 40 plus years of marriage. I began to realize how the book captured a lifetime of skills developed in my careers as a psychologist and professional coach. It is also a chronicle of my own personal journey to self fulfillment. By promoting your growth as well as offering communication and interpersonal strategies, I hope to empower each of you to create more personal happiness in a loving relationship... with yourself and others.

The work is derived from a heart of love and my knowledge as an mental, emotional, and spiritual guide. May your relationships continue to grow into healthier, more vibrant, loving, joyful ones, and you can become more closely connected with all who are dear to you. Most importantly, may you continue to grow in your own awareness of your feelings that you are indeed unique and precious. May you also continue to practice conscious loving. After all, true love starts within you, my dearest reader. May you treasure your greatest gifts—you, and your ever-expanding ability to love.

January

JANUARY 1

New Beginnings

> **Our love is just the beginning.**

As we start each New Year, we face the future with a fresh approach. **Today is the new beginning of our love.** We plan to create special events to help transform our love to a greater closeness, commitment, happiness, and fulfillment. We start the new year with a commitment to make each day memorable in the ways we communicate and express our love. We may renew our wedding vows to love, honor, protect, and cherish the other or we may read this book together and engage in the suggested activities. "You are the most precious person in the entire world to me. I love you eternally."

JANUARY 2

Writing Daily Notes Of Love

Each day we write a message of love that is recorded in a notebook.

Days too quickly melt into weeks, months, and all too soon ,years. We commemorate and chronicle our relationship by writing down our thoughts, perceptions, emotions, and poems… all of which we want to share with each other. This loving act could be at night when we each contemplate what we mean to each other, allowing us to see a beautiful message by our beloved first thing in the morning. This could also be written in the quiet of the morning, when we feel fresh with inspiration and appreciation for each other. In this notebook, we can write responses to one another or express a completely different thought or emotion. **Today we commit to daily sharing our thoughts of love.**

JANUARY 3

Past And Present

We travel side by side on our journey to exquisite love.

Often to know where we are going, it is necessary to look back from where we came. **Today we remember so many treasured moments we've experienced during this past year as we look at our past together.** Did these tender memories result from an unusual hardship or a peak time of fun and light heartedness? What made these events so memorable to us? What were some special words we recalled? Perhaps there were various expressions on our faces of glee, amazement, and affection we remember. Was there a particular touch, a notable loving gesture, or a remarkable harmonic time of playing and working together we recall? We discuss each of these things, uncovering the unique people we are. It helps us to better know ourselves as individuals. By conversing, we learn what we each hold sacred about the other. We can be catalysts to make our love blossom. We can assist each other to be the best possible self by examining our past so we can identify and expand these experiences to enjoy even more love.

JANUARY 4

How Are You?

> **I ask, "How are you?" You reply, "I'm so in love with you!**

Your response warms my heart and lights my spirit each time I hear your words. I never before realized I would experience the immense joy and spontaneous affection that clearly speak volumes of your passion and commitment to me. No one has ever treated me so tenderly and lovingly before. I want to be kind, thoughtful, gentle and creative in returning my love to you. You deserve the best life has to offer; the best I can offer. **The next time you ask how I'm doing, I reply, "I'm so in love with you!"**

JANUARY 5

Blessings

> **I count my blessings each time I awaken to you.**

You are the first person I awaken to each morning and the last person I want to see before I drift off to sleep at night. I've never considered myself a morning person, yet when I wake up next to you, I am so happy you are here by my side. I count my blessings. What a wonderful way to start each day! When I view our beautiful environment, whether the sun is shining and flooding our room with cheerfulness and optimism for a new day—or cloudy and rainy with thunder and lightning, I am eager to start our adventure together. Finally, at the end of the day, nothing could be sweeter than to kiss and hold you. I gaze upon you one last time before I close my eyes, feel your body, and hear your rhythmic breathing. **Today and every day, as I awaken to you, I count you as my most precious blessing.** Thank you, my dearest one, for being in my life.

JANUARY 6

Surprise

Today I willingly initiate a gesture of my love and devotion.

Often your thoughts and actions fill me with such a deep sense of awe, wonder, and gratitude. You may be softly awakening me with a kiss or making coffee for us in the morning without a complaint. Other ways you show me love include washing the car, taking me to my favorite restaurant, or sensing my thoughts and feelings. Each word and gesture is pure joy. **Today I consciously store these true gifts in my heart and initiate a loving act to show my love, devotion, and appreciation**. For instance, when you awaken there is fresh coffee waiting for you with your favorite breakfast, clothes are neatly laid out for an outing, bags have already been packed in the car, or a lunch or takeaway bag is filled with goodies... a love note tucked inside, or perhaps a secret destination is in store for you.

JANUARY 7

First Meeting

We take a moment to remember when, where, and how we met.

I can remember the moment my eyes first met yours. As you started speaking, I found myself completely spellbound by your humor, wit, and attractiveness. You piqued my interest; my excitement and intrigue grew. Our first meeting is reborn as we talk about how we met and the qualities that drew us to each other. Thank you, God, for bringing me your greatest gift... a soul mate who provides me with total unconditional love! **Today we discuss how we met and the moment your eyes met mine.** How do we feel, what do we think, and what do we see and hear as we relive our beginning together?

JANUARY 8

Acceptance

To love you is to accept you just the way you are.

I can show my love to you in the deepest way by allowing you to be you. Your unimitable personality is the very reason that I was originally attracted to you. You are perfect the way you are. I love you even when I try to change you. Each time I find myself trying to change you, I remind myself that I was attracted to you just the way you are. **Today I rediscover and redefine how cherished you are to me by reminding myself to suspend my judgment to better appreciate the person that you are.** I can then notice your uniqueness.

JANUARY 9

Kissing

I give you a soulful kiss.

A quick peck here and there doesn't do. Today we playfully and sensually give the other long, lingering kisses. Can we do this for 30 seconds, even one minute? We sense the way we wrap our arms around each other, and how our lips, mouths, and tongues meet, exploring ways to show our affection even more. I leave for the day with your sweet kiss upon my lips. **Today and every day, we take the time to give each other a passionate kiss... just like fingerprints, no two kisses are alike!**

JANUARY 10

Listening

Carefully listening and understanding are the richest gifts we can give to each other.

You don't have to agree with me or like my feelings. However, I do need you to actively listen with your eyes, ears, and heart to my exuberance—and to my joys, sadness, fears, anger, hurts, and disappointments. When you truly hear and understand my thoughts and feeling by repeating them in your own words, I know that you are validating and emotionally supporting me. These revered times are when I feel the closest and most intimate with you. **Today we practice taking turns talking and carefully listening to each other as we repeat the other's thoughts and feelings.**

JANUARY 11

Loving Self

Today I reflect on the qualities I love about myself.

It is important that I take time to examine and write the behaviors and characteristics I like and love about myself. I know that unless I can love myself, I cannot truly love anyone else. Otherwise, I would look to you to confirm my own existence and worthiness. I acknowledge the unfairness of my demands for you to love me, to accept me, and to make me happy and whole. I realize that I can be proud of who I am, which is important to my own self-esteem. My esteem and the essence of my success are not limited to career or financial achievements. Too often we criticize ourselves for falling short of reaching our own expectations. **Today I celebrate my own being as I look back from where I came and see the growth I've experienced. By loving myself, I can now more fully love you.**

JANUARY 12

Quality Of Time

It is not the amount of time spent with you; rather how our time is spent together.

We have often described our weekends as idyllic honeymoons since we spend so much time apart in working away from home. Whenever we finally are together, we value our limited time, talking, laughing, having fun, and loving each other. I want to spend our times together, as if every moment is precious and may disappear all too suddenly. **Today I make you my priority by giving you my complete focus.** My dearest, I want to give you my total undivided attention to enhance our time together. If you ever sense I am not, please gently remind me by kissing me and whispering in my ear that you want my attention.

JANUARY 13

Anger

Arguments let us know the other's deepest hurts and disappointments.

Despite the fact disagreements can be disruptive and create a degree of anguish, they can also be beneficial. We can allow them to become an outlet for disappointments, fears, differences, frustrations, and hurts—or even just how we view situations differently. The next time we have a disagreement, I promise to listen to you to discover how you think and feel. I often remind myself your feelings do make sense when I listen with compassion and remain nonjudgmental. I communicate to you that I do understand what you said by stating in my own words your feelings and the reasons behind your feelings and actions. **Today I listen for other emotions hiding beneath your anger, so I can better understand your thoughts, feelings and actions.**

JANUARY 14

Weekly Dates

Our relationship is a priority.

Our relationship can become lost inside the busy day-to-day activities, as we work, perform tasks at home and take care of our family. ***Today we set a weekly date to keep our relationship fun and alive.*** Unless we take the time to care for our relationship, we allow events to control our lives. Having a weekly date permits us to have something to look forward to when we go through our week. We discuss and plan where we will go, and what we can do this weekend. I'm looking forward to having time alone with you.

JANUARY 15

Communication

From the beginning we talked and talked and talked.

Fleeting moments evaporated too quickly as minutes, then hours left us longing for more time together. We had so much to say to each other, especially in the beginning of our relationship. Now after all these years, we are still filled with ideas and feelings eagerly waiting to be expressed. **Today we talk as if we're getting to know each other for the first time.** We talk about the qualities that make us stand out, our passions and interests, and our concepts of our ideal mate, values, and important influences from family. We also discuss lighter topics we clearly enjoy such as sports, food, current events, politics, or our favorite ways to relax, smile, giggle, and remain steadfastly connected.

JANUARY 16

Self Nurturing

> ### The greatest gift I can give to myself and my loved ones is to gently and consistently meet my own needs.

Because far too many of us are taught not to be selfish, we often neglect our own needs and wants, and unwisely put the needs of others before us. This practice actually harms us by robbing us of our energy, joy and self-care. Thus, I remind myself to be mindfully aware of my needs and know that it is healthy for me to put myself first. By taking care of myself, I give an incredible gift to all those around me by being happier and more pleasant to be around. I also free others of the responsibility of taking care of my needs. **Today and every day, I give myself permission to meet my own needs by prioritizing myself.** I can thereby give myself love, which then spreads to those around me.

JANUARY 17

Awareness

> ### Change begins with my awareness.

I immediately communicate with you regarding any specific actions or comments that hurt, sadden, or anger me. When I am direct and specific about your behaviors while remaining calm, I enhance the chances of a positive outcome for both of us. If I hold in my feelings, convincing myself that "it's no big deal," they continue to fester over time resulting in a major explosion over a minor incident. When I am aware of my emotions blowing out of proportion, I realize my reaction is from the past as well as the present. **Today I pledge to communicate with you as I become aware of my feelings, and I calmly do so shortly after it happens.**

JANUARY 18

Reminiscing Through Photographs

Looking through photographs together reminds us of the many joys we've shared.

We share so very many beautiful memories paging through the photographs of our lives—frequently taking notice of how young and carefree we appear in our pictures. We remember and discuss the places we have been—and the sights, conversations, and special moments that have touched us. How amazing we have thus recorded the story of our lives. Here is our love story unfolding and deepening with its many twists and turns. We've experienced such phenomenal happiness through many adventures, and discoveries together. All of these experiences have enhanced our passion for each other and for life. **Today we leaf through the photographs of our lives, relating experiences and feelings as we bond our past, present and future together.**

JANUARY 19

Healing

I examine my wounds from my past to begin my emotional healing.

Too often we carry emotional "baggage," about which we may feel a sense of shame that erodes confidence and esteem. Additionally, our shame can surface whenever we experience events that lead us to feel inadequate, less than, different from others, and unworthy. Today I look inward and examine the source of my shame so I can begin to heal. Perhaps it was from growing up poor, looking different in some way, struggling with school, or living in a family where there were problems with chemical dependency, abuse—or perhaps just not receiving demonstrations of verbal or physical signs of affection. **Today I take the first step by identifying my sources of shame, and I affirm to help the child in me grow to become healthy, to feel worthy, and commit to re-parenting myself with nurturing, love, and support to be all that I can be.**

JANUARY 20

Roses On The Pillow

Romance is created by our imagination.

No matter how financially rich or poor we may be, we can be rich in our imaginations. We can choose to create romance by just thinking and acting upon what might please our loved one. Candles diffusing an irresistible fragrance can help create a romantic mood. Similarly, a dinner at home or in a restaurant, eaten in a relaxing manner, during which time you "eat me with your eyes," can express the most endearing messages to me. A simple note on the bathroom counter to be viewed first thing in the morning, the unexpected message in my lunch bag, or the act of spreading flower petals or chocolate Hershey Kisses on our bed say "I love you." I am indeed rich in love. **Today I use my creativity to show you a way of demonstrating my love for you.**

JANUARY 21

Teaching

Teaching a loved one a skill is an act of love and patience.

The thought of teaching you to ski filled me with great excitement to be able to introduce you to the exhilarating thrill of gliding down mountainsides, feeling weightless and free. I took time to coach you on the techniques and you were a receptive student, listening attentively and doing your best to follow my instructions. We took it one step at a time until you could stand up on your own and begin to carve your turns in the snow. I felt like a proud parent, my heart singing with joy. Thank you for your commitment to learn a skill that is important to me. **Today I commit to learning a skill or activity that brings enjoyment to you.**

JANUARY 22

Gatherings

You whisper words of love when we're in a crowd.

No matter the size of our social gatherings, sometime during a long evening you whisper, "You are the most beautiful woman in the room." Your words are magical to me. After all these years, we do still consider each other to be physically attractive despite our changes in appearance. We are not perfect, but you are by far, the most attractive person to me. We are seeing with our hearts. How sweet to know you find me so appealing. **The next time we are at a gathering, I tell you, with a smile and look of adoration, that you are absolutely the most irresistible and attractive person in the room**.

JANUARY 23

Patience

Love is patient. Love is allowing you to find your own answers.

Love takes the time to listen, to learn, and to support. Love waits for you to discover and determine your own solutions, and not be pressured by my ideas for the way you might solve your problems. Although I continually want the best for you and am filled with the best intentions, my verbal responses to you may not be what you want to hear from me. You may think I am not taking enough time listening to you, or prematurely being too focused on your taking action in the ways I believe are appropriate for you. You are the expert on what is the right solution for you. **Today I ask you to please communicate with me directly if I am too pushy with solutions or advice for you. Indeed, you do have the best solutions within you, and I want to respect this.**

JANUARY 24

Sharing Responsibilities

Any household responsibilities are easier with you by my side.

No matter how mundane the task, each project seems to go faster and smoother when we work together. I still remember when we were in college, how sitting next to you while we studied brought such rich anticipation and excitement. When we do yard work together, or when we clean the house, these chores seem to speed by with our involvement. Our conversations and unity of effort fortify us while we tidy our home and landscape. **Today we share a task we've been putting off and recapture the romance and commitment to each other by becoming engrossed in conversation while we work together.** We look on these tasks as a life process. We can become energized simply by working together while accomplishing everyday chores.

JANUARY 25

Seduction

I want to make your heart flutter with my eyes.

How long has it been since I've seduced you? When we were dating, we'd playfully bat our eyes at each other, allowing the other to notice just how interested we were. You'd flirt and tease with your lashes and kisses, starting at my cheeks and ears—seeking your way down my neck, sending shivers of excitement down my spine and giving me goose bumps. You'd love the way you could elicit such immediate reactions. Almost simultaneously, I would whisper softly in your ears, my warm breath producing low moans of ecstasy from you. **Today we practice the art of seduction, learning even more ways to arouse the fire of love.**

JANUARY 26

Physical Attention

Today is for loving and honoring our bodies.

We may sometimes think we must have sex in order to feel connected with one another. **Today we take quality time to become re-acquainted with our bodies, and how we react to each other's touch.** We take turns massaging each other, noting when the other relaxes and breathes deeply and slowly, and when our respiration quickens or our muscles tighten. We are vulnerable and open. We cherish getting to know our bodies and pleasuring each other without sex, allowing us to just enjoy and relax, reveling in the sensations.

JANUARY 27

Dance

Slow dancing with you is nostalgic and allows me to feel close to you.

We pick some of our favorite tunes, wrap our arms around each other, and sway slowly to the music. Then we dreamily close our eyes and imagine ourselves in a ballroom, listening to the sounds and noticing only the rhythm of our bodies. We match the other's steps and movements as we seemingly float away together. If we are jarred back to reality by the stepping on the other's toes, we giggle and capitalize on the moment. **Today we dance to the music—creating fun, romance, laughter and memories.**

JANUARY 28

Tears

Sometimes your tender acts of love can touch me with tears.

When tears flow, my emotions are pure. Sometimes the ways you look at me, hold me, and speak to me, move me to heartfelt tears of happiness. At times, I feel overwhelmed that I could be married to someone who is as unbelievably wonderful as you. We allow ourselves to recall and speak about a previous endearing event. For example, even when your funds were limited in college, you would stop by the campus greenhouse and select a handful of roses to delight me. My heart would melt. **Today, I allow myself to remember and express a tender gesture which moved me by the way you expressed your love.**

JANUARY 29

Personal Time

We deeply love ourselves and each other by creating personal time.

Sometimes the best way to show how much you love me is by allowing me to have my own space and time. Perhaps this is so I can be with my friends or family. Other times, it's allowing me to be alone and indulging in a long, luxurious nap on the weekends. You might have taken care of our child while I slept, exercised, or leisurely read the newspaper. By having my own personal time to rejuvenate, I am refreshed—now more fully able to be with you. **Today we give each other the gift of personal time to use as we wish.**

JANUARY 30

Connectedness

No matter how tired you are when my body touches yours, you turn towards me.

As you sleep, your body slowly gravitates toward mine, and you reach for my face, my hand, or my chest as we snuggle closer. As completely as the pieces of a puzzle—we fit oh! so perfectly together. Even in your sleep you whisper words of love as I come to bed. Thank you, my darling. We are truly one. **Tonight we consciously nestle together as we fall asleep.**

JANUARY 31

Communication

Communication keeps us connected.

From the very beginning, our relationship was based on our having great conversations. When we are so enveloped in our thoughts and words, we forget the passage of time. Each day brings a discovery of thoughts, feelings, and dreams. Our thoughts flow like a stream bursting with a life force that vitalizes and clarifies. **Today we take time to truly communicate our dreams and emotions.** We might discuss the goals we want to accomplish together this week, this month, or this year. Instead of just making a list of things we must accomplish, we share our responses and feel the synergy of our minds and affection. Let's steal time to talk together. Moments like these are kept forever as we grow even closer together.

february

FEBRUARY 1

Whispering Sweet Somethings

> **Nothing is better than your whispering words of love in my ear.**

There are certain times when you are especially tender and softly voice small appreciations such as my smelling good, the smoothness of my skin, how much you enjoyed the meal I prepared or the work I did in our home. You whisper "sweet somethings" to help encourage me, and I respond by drawing my body close to you. You are still able to make my heart jump when I hear your words of endearment and appreciation. **Today we reveal at least one thing we appreciate about the other.**

FEBRUARY 2

Morning Showers

What a wonderful way of starting the day together.

Showering together in the mornings is a way of sharing myself with you and starting the day together. We take turns lathering each other. How silly we are, yet how fully in tune with our bodies as we playfully reach out to scrub each other's backs. Life's simple pleasures when you put lotion on my back or give me a hug from behind accompanied by "Guess who?" are indelibly etched on my mind. **Today we commit to taking showers together whenever possible as a means to indulge each other with a loving touch and playfulness.**

FEBRUARY 3

Sameness

We are so different, yet when we are together, we often seem to be the same.

We regularly think alike, often using the same phrases or explanations. How amazing that the other knows what is going to be said and thinks of the same exact words, literally milliseconds before the other states them. This is remarkable since we not only may finish each other sentences, but possess similar values, goals, and interests despite the fact we grew up separately with very different family backgrounds. You are definitely my equal and my soul mate. **Today we list and discuss our similarities, knowing that we were truly meant for each other.**

FEBRUARY 4

Pampering

You pamper me with hot tea and chocolates.

I feel as if I am the luckiest person in the world when you ask me if you can bring me a cup of hot tea and chocolates from the kitchen. At the end of a long day of work, relaxing in front of the television, or being on the Internet, you say those magical words, "Could I get you some hot tea and chocolates?" I immediately thank you and feel grateful. Your considerate acts of love cost nothing, yet mean everything to me. Now, how about some popcorn for you? **I take pleasure in pampering you today.**

FEBRUARY 5

Celebration

Every day together is a celebration of joy and love.

Although today is not a special holiday, it is still a celebratory occasion, as is every precious day we spend our together. **Today I take time to find a moment to reflect how we can use this time to consciously make our love and experiencies more meaningful.** Do we enjoy a favorite meal together, plant another flower or bush to commemorate our unity, hike our favorite trail to the top of the mountain, or simply stroll and admire our beautiful garden we lovingly and painstakingly planted side by side?

FEBRUARY 6

Openness

We enhance our love by being open to all possibilities.

We are continually provided important information about each other's thoughts and actions. However, we may not consciously listen to all the facts; making assumptions that could potentially cause damage to our relationship through false conclusions and preconceived ideas of how the other thinks, feels or acts in a particular manner. We may become guarded and defensive, protecting and justifying our own feelings and behaviors. Conversely—if we listen with our ears and heart, we can be open to all possibilities. We can do this by repeating in our own words each other's feelings and the reasons behind those feelings. **Today, by simply listening and really hearing each other, we learn of the other's thoughts, feelings, and needs.** We can now fully understand the other's intentions and actions, deepening our love and respect for one another. We begin to feel truly understood and valued because we are heard and appreciated.

FEBRUARY 7

Being Apart

When we're apart, I can hear your voice and picture your gestures and facial expressions.

Your image brings a smile to my face and my body relaxes. We stay in touch with e-mails, text messages, or loving phone calls, and hurried notes scribbled on scraps of paper. I can feel your love, because no matter where you are, I think of you, and I know that you, too, are thinking of me. **Today we commit that whenever we are apart, we send signs of our love such as notes and phone calls to those we cherish.**

FEBRUARY 8

A Mirror To My Soul

When irritated about your behaviors, I look inside myself to find the source of the disturbance.

You serve as the mirror to my soul... a type of barometer that reflects whether I'm happy and content as well as my anger and frustration. By looking inward, I may find there is something I do not like about myself which I am unable to see or accept. Instead I may blame my shortcomings on you; accusing you of being too critical when that is the very behavior I am exhibiting. I now realize by rectifying what is causing me pain and unhappiness, I may become more accepting and loving towards you. **Today I look into myself first to truly discover the source of my own hurt, sadness, disappointment, and anger, to circumvent reflexively lashing out at you.**

FEBRUARY 9

Calm

When we are stressed, we take time to regain a sense of calm.

We may be unable to understand or have compassion for each other if we are angry, sad, stressed, or anxious. In order to accept how the other is feeling, we may need to take a "time out" to restore our own sense of calmness. We might ask ourselves how we are thinking and feeling, sometimes writing these down to further examine and release on paper. By allowing our emotions to settle in a more beneficial direction, we may more easily discern different perspectives. When we find a change in view from our original perspective and feelings, we can more easily show empathy and caring for each other. By becoming more in tune with the intensity of our emotions, we take personal responsibility in safeguarding them. **Today we commit to taking time out whenever our emotions become unmanageable—to restore a sense of calm and to enable us to view situations and intentions of our partner in a better light.**

FEBRUARY 10

Personal Best

You bring out the best in me.

Whenever we are together, you bring out the finest qualities in me. I want to be the best person, mate, friend, and lover to you. I want to show you how much you mean to me each moment we are together. My spirits are higher, and I smile and laugh. I absolutely adore you! I want to work on projects to help you succeed and accomplish your goals. I want to please you in every way; not because I need to, but because it brings me such happiness. I see and feel you beam with delight. **Today we discuss how we bring out the best in each other... and ourselves.**

FEBRUARY 11

Game Time

I'm going to give you a run for your money.

When it comes to games, we've both met our match. In fact, we frequently joke, "you are a worthy adversary." Our board and card games are true bouts between competitors, never really knowing who is going to be the winner until the very end. Until we met, I never knew games could be so much fun. We can easily be transported back to our childhoods—creating playfulness no matter how old we are. **Let's play a board game or some cards today!**

FEBRUARY 12

Appreciation

I celebrate my appreciation of you.

Today, I show my love, deep affection, and appreciation for your many gifts and talents. I take time to tell you at least one particular attribute or action I admire about you. These compliments and acknowledgements open the way for spontaneous emotional and physical demonstrations of love. I love your positive energy and how you consistently encourage me to pursue my dreams. I delight in your warm embrace. How close we have become over the years. I love the way you are my biggest supporter with whom I can confide in during the best and worst of times. Even when I make a mistake which leads me to misfortunes, you are there by my side, encouraging me without any signs of criticism. For that, I am eternally grateful, my love.

FEBRUARY 13

Signs Of Love

Your love can be a glance, a touch, a smile, or encouraging words that ease my days.

Your love reaches out to me in so many different ways each day. For example, on your way home, you ask if I need anything from the store. You stop and notice my favorite pastry, and later present me with a kiss and a sweet dessert. You even get up before the crack of dawn to join me in an activity which tests your patience. The various things you do are endless, yet the meaning is perfectly clear: "I love you." **Today I perform an act of love especially for you.**

FEBRUARY 14

Valentine's Day

**Please be mine—
today and every day.**

Valentine's Day is our day to celebrate love. It's not the typical chocolate candy or the romantic dinner that sets my heart racing. Rather, it's you who leaves me breathless with your daily acts of kindness, warm thoughts, demonstrations of affection, and impeccably steadfast... all encompassing devotion. I love you for loving me so completely and unconditionally. I am fulfilled. **Today we celebrate Valentine's Day by engaging in a romantic act that is creative, memorable, and fun for both.** For instance, I might instruct you to be ready at 5 p.m. and pick you up for our date in a chauffeur outfit. Then I blindfold you and kiss your hands, neck, ears, and face. You are then whisked away to a place which has a special significance for us—to have a gourmet picnic. This place may even be at home with a picnic basket and favorite blankets and cushions already spread out so we can lustily eat and feast the eyes. Oh, did I mention that there is nothing there between that chauffeur outfit and me? Valentine, please be mine forever.

FEBRUARY 15

Others

Allowing others into our lives enriches our own.

My life was enriched as I engaged in conversation with a unique individual possessing incredible insights, who pressed me to define my goals. In our daily lives, those insights may be a simple observation, a comment, or a spontaneous hug by a relative, friend or acquaintance. Unexpectedly, another person can teach us a lesson about life or a skill we wish to develop. Sometimes it is those chance meetings from a stranger or a new acquaintance that can suddenly change the course of our lives. We are enlightened and may feel such a strong spiritual connection, that we are changed forever. **Today and every day we open our friendship to those who touch us with their sincerity, consideration, and the magnetic draw of their unique abilities**. We are also aware of the possibility of how others can enrich our lives when they give us words of encouragement. They inspire us through their wisdom and actions, helping us to have greater insight, as they display love and kindness.

FEBRUARY 16

Accepting

I couldn't ask for anything more than to snuggle next to you on a cold winter night.

It's cold outside and I come to bed with cold feet and hands. I snuggle next to you seeking warmth. You don't turn me away or chide me about being too cold. Instead you turn towards me and share your body heat, allowing our bodies to merge into one. You radiate acceptance and your love envelopes me. I am relaxed and easily fall asleep with a smile on my face. **Tonight our bodies intertwine together, sharing our warmth and comfort, secure in our love.**

FEBRUARY 17

Excitement

When you come home, I show you unconditional love.

When you come home, I have this exhilarating sense of wanting to show the same type of unconditional love and body-wiggling excitement as our dog displays to us. I want to race to you, jump into your arms, and give you a "Where have you been?" type of hug and kiss. **Today I show you my love, anticipation, and excitement as soon as you walk through the door. Welcome home! I am so happy to see you!**

FEBRUARY 18

Listening

Love speaks strongest when we allow ourselves to listen with our ears, heart, and total being.

Your love has often touched me when you have spoken openly about your most private feelings. These secrets seem to flow so easily. You freely display your trust and affection for me by confiding in me. Other times your love has made its greatest impact when you simply held me or rubbed my back while you listened to me. I love you for these gestures of being totally present without offering any advice or solutions. **Today we take the time to fully listen with our eyes and ears, and include touching each other as we give undivided attention to one another.**

FEBRUARY 19

Prayers

Before I met you, I prayed for you.

Somehow, I instinctively knew that you were out there in this vast universe. I prayed that God would bless you, care for you, and keep you safe, while gently wrapping His arms around you until I could. God answered my prayers the day we met and has continued to do so each day thereafter. You are indeed a gift from the heavens. My heart overflows with joy and gratitude. May God in His goodness continue to watch over you. **Today we express gratitude to God or a spiritual higher power for His blessings to us and the world.**

FEBRUARY 20

Walks

The simple act of walking side by side is a powerful metaphor which speaks of you and me.

Walking brought us closer together when we first met. It allowed us to become captivated with each other during simpler times when we had few material objects to give. We offered the other not only our hearts, but our intellect, our energy, our creativity, and our total being. Walking together hand in hand gave us the time to really know and understand each other; falling in love with the real person without the fantasies of fame or fortune. **Today, we recreate those loving, exciting discoveries by walking hand in hand again and sharing our dreams and our feelings towards the other.**

FEBRUARY 21

Anger

Time is too precious to stay angry.

Time spent with you is much too short. I want every minute of our time to be close and full of affection. Whenever we have had arguments, I feel sad our harmony has been disrupted. We typically feel attacked and criticized when the other denigrates our character rather than describing the behaviors causing the problem. We both have the need to discuss our thoughts, feelings, and the problematic actions to fully resolve our differences. We both can have our own feelings and still show each other emotional understanding and support without having to be right. **Today I suspend my anger and criticalness and commit myself to truly listening to your thoughts and feelings**.

FEBRUARY 22

Love Letters

Today I write a love letter to my precious one.

How long has it been since I've written a love letter to the person that is dearest to me? When we were dating, we would frequently send cards and letters professing our love for each other. Over time, these outward expressions of love diminished. **Today, I write a letter to remind both of us how loved you are, and how I am the most fortunate person in this world. Love and kisses forever!**

FEBRUARY 23

Home

Together we have built our home.

We planned our home from beginning to end. Our home became our symbol of love... a peaceful, tranquil retreat from the frantic pace of our modern world. As we gaze inside and outside our home, we are filled with gratitude and wonderment at our many blessings and the beauty of our love nest. We never tire of coming home to our castle—our unique place of quiet repose, fun, festivities, and renewable energy. Thank you, my love, for the gift of a magnificent home that we've created. **Today we take the time to appreciate our beautiful home and surroundings.**

FEBRUARY 24

Hobbies

We undertake a hobby or interest.

Today we discuss and explore any interests we may want to pursue. That interest could be taking a golf lesson, perhaps trying different gym equipment, joining a new church, or giving each other a leisurely massage. We express interests such as photography, playing guitar, painting, pottery, learning a new language, or getting back to a long forgotten activity such as fishing, biking, roller blading, or simply reading or singing to each other. It's up to us to keep our relationship fun and new. **Today we start a new pursuit or revisit an old activity together.**

FEBRUARY 25

Everyday Gestures

You call to let me know you're on your way.

One way we can consciously show our consideration and love for one another is by calling to give an estimated time of arrival or to update any deviances from a planned routine. When I hear from you, I am comforted by the knowledge you are safe and returning to me. Your keeping me informed of your status is a loving gesture that certainly is recognized and appreciated. **Today we speak about the little gestures and acts of kindness that contribute to our closeness and love.**

FEBRUARY 26

Support

Whatever your goals for home or work, I want to be your greatest supporter.

When you share with me the goals you'd like to attain, I feel included and closer to you. You may have a presentation to give… perhaps a stressful event approaching, and I eagerly listen to you while we brainstorm and strategize about how to succeed. So frequently our discussions have clarified the directions we take. Thank you for sharing your goals, visions, and conflicts and for being there when I share mine. **Today we discuss a goal that you'd like to achieve; we define what it is, why it's important to you, and establish action steps and deadlines for achieving success.**

FEBRUARY 27

Flowers

Flowers are the language of love.

You're coming back from a business trip and are tired and eager to come home. Yet you take time to stop and bring me home a beautiful bouquet of flowers. Your loving behavior shows me clearly just how much you've missed me. I can't thank or love you enough. **Today we show our love by giving our dear one a gift as a token of our affection and admiration.**

FEBRUARY 28

Sexual Playfulness

We have such fun times when we have sexual intimacy.

Sometimes the best times are before the commencement of the act of love when we can be silly or do an erotic or comedic strip tease. Other times we actually burst out laughing during or after sex when we playfully joke. This can be the most hilarious when we are relaxed and can be our spontaneous, frivolous selves. Let's keep the humor and the fun in our sex life! **Today we interject playfulness and fun into our sexual intimacy.**

FEBRUARY 29

Dreams

**You are the
one I love.**

You are even more wonderful than I ever imagined in my dreams. You are real, not an illusion that appears and is gone tomorrow. For you see, I am wide awake! On this earth, I am free to dream of you both day and night, caught in the reverie of our miraculous love. You consistently show me so many ways of demonstrating love through your words, deeds, and touch. **Today I tell you that you are even better than in my dreams***!*

march

Music

Music helps us to express our sentiments to each other.

You love to listen to music, whether you are working or relaxing. When we go on trips, you carefully choose the music to match our moods or setting. By listening and discussing music, we find another way to add vibrancy to our lives. We can generate excitement and energy or choose music selections that are soothing and calming. **Today we select music together and listen to the songs as we are wrapped in each other's warm embrace.**

MARCH 2

Spooning

Lying next to you, I can feel your breath and the beating of your heart.

One of our most enjoyable times is when our bodies overlap, lying next to each other on a comfy sofa as we watch our favorite television shows or indulge in a nap. I am fulfilled and content—shutting out the day, absorbed in our moment, when I can feel the love your body emenates. I notice how perfectly our bodies fit together. Your energy synergistically increases mine as we cheer for our favorite teams. How exciting it is to watch a thrilling, adrenaline producing movie with us snuggled together or nestled as one by the fireplace. **Today we lie close to each other while we share an activity, taking time to simply unwind, rejuvenate, and be in tune with the other's breath.**

MARCH 3

Self-Inventory

Today I examine any shortcomings and shame that I may carry.

Until I am willing to truly recognize, acknowledge, and own weaknesses I may hold, I cannot improve or learn to genuinely love myself. Indeed, I keep repeating past self-defeating behaviors – hoping for a different outcome. When I look at myself in an uncritical and honest way, I ask myself this question, "Am I doing the best I can to be the person I want to be?" When I uncover the qualities and behaviors that are harmful to our relationship or to me, I commit to taking steps to change them. As I become emotionally healthier, I no longer carry vestiges of shame which weigh down my self-confidence and esteem. When I carry shame, I am self-conscious and inadequate, looking towards others to make me feel whole. As I identify and release my shame by fully believing in my own self-worth, my loving self-acceptance frees me to raise my love for you to higher, purer level. **Today I examine my shortcomings and shame to overcome the barriers which prevent me from fully loving myself and you.**

MARCH 4

Sipping And Sharing

Sharing our food or drink are metaphors for our daily giving and receiving from each other.

When we go out to eat, instead of sitting apart from each other, we make sure to cozily sit together, frequently offering the other a tasty bite of food or the first sampling of beverage. Our communal sharing has become an established pattern for throughout the day. It could be offering a bite of a decadent dessert at home or a fragrant cup of coffee. It could also mean sharing a blanket as we seek to warm our bodies while huddling in the winter months in front of the television or while reading together. **Today we enjoy the loving act of sharing, giving, and receiving.**

MARCH 5

Worship

We pray to God and thank Him for our blessings and His grace.

We often think of Easter and Christmas as the holidays to attend special church services. However, the daily power of using prayer and positive intentions feeds our souls and those of others… including our circle of friends and family. By being aligned with daily gratitude and prayer, we are able to more easily get through each day, as well as feeling linked with those important to us. **Today we say a prayer for our families, our friends, ourselves, and all those on earth so they can experience the uplifting joys, love, and blessings that we share.** We express our thanks and extend blessings to all those in our hearts and minds today and every day.

MARCH 6

Esteem

> **My esteem is manifested in how much I am able to love myself.**

Without having self-esteem, I am unable to completely love myself. Nor am I able to fully love anyone else, because I would not be confident or like myself. Instead, I would be needy of your love, attention, and admiration which you would not be able to fulfill. I would be pressing you to give me even more of your love until you felt drained and smothered. **Today, I consciously affirm my self worth by listing the qualities I value in myself—to more easily allow you to cherish me.** Only when I honestly think and feel I am worthy, I can then believe and accept your own compliments and physical demonstrations of affection as legitimate.

MARCH 7

Kissing

> **Kissing at the movies, while holding hands and leaning toward the other, is both sensual and playful**

Remember when we were still in high school and never wanted our parents around so, we could kiss and hug during the movies? We re-play some of those frisky behaviors, feeling oh, so naughty and thinking we've gotten away with something. You still thrill me now as you did when we were first dating—kissing, hugging, and clutching each other during those scary and action-packed adrenaline rush scenes. **Today we are nostalgic as we cuddle together and kiss at the movies or at home, watching a favorite program.**

MARCH 8

Scavenger Hunt

We create fun and excitement through our imagination.

Daily routines can dull the fun, playfulness, and excitement in our lives. Recalling how we grabbed colored eggs from their hiding spots as children, we decide to organize a scavenger hunt using love notes instead of eggs. **Today we playfully take turns hiding notes and giving verbal and physical clues to guide each other to the ultimate goal... love.**

MARCH 9

Giving And Receiving Compliments

Love is reflected in every action we take.

Today I am committed to recognizing the behaviors and characteristics I most often admire in you by praising at least one thing about you. I do not want to become critical, or lose sight of your gifts and the many strengths you possess. When I verbally praise you, I remind myself of all those qualities I love about you and the actions that show your tender, fun, and caring sides. When I take time to compliment you, I can sense your enthusiasm, appreciation, and love—encouraging me even more to look for your qualities that I value so much. In turn, you compliment and acknowledge my actions, enhancing our circle of love.

MARCH 10

Requesting Changes In Behavior

I make direct requests of you to show my love and respect for both you and me.

Whenever I am assertive and I express certain behavior changes I'd like from you, my chances of being even happier dramatically increase, because I am being honest and clear about my needs and wishes. When you listen to my wishes and consider them, I know that you love me enough to examine your own behavior and to empathize with my feelings. By making specific requests, I avoid my attempt to manipulate, control, or overpower you. Instead, I allow you to choose change because you want to and not because you should or must give in to keep the peace. Thank you for listening to my needs. **Today I directly express a need or wish for a particular behavior from you, stating,**

"I would appreciate if you would _____.

This is important to me, because _____.

When you do _____(specifically stating the other's undesirable or old behavior), then I feel _____, because _____.

Thank you for listening to my request."

43

MARCH 11

Sleeping Late

I want to linger in bed with you.

It's idyllic to leisurely snuggle and cling to each other on the weekends. Sometimes you will mischievously torture me when I must get ready for work. You pull me closer to you during the work week and beg me not to leave you. During the weekend, it's so refreshing when we both can sleep in and watch the sun streaming through our bedroom windows. **Today we spend the morning in bed, lazily stretching, kissing, talking, reading the newspaper, sipping coffee, and falling back to sleep.**

MARCH 12

Roles And Communication

We communicate in an adult- to- adult manner by expressing our thoughts, feelings and needs.

Sometimes when we talk to each other, I talk to you as a parent to a child. When I am judgmental, critical, blaming, commanding, and ordering, you might respond like a rebellious youngster who is filled with anger and fury, ready to attack or to justify your actions. It is at times like these we remind ourselves that either of us has the power to change emotionally charged interactions at any given time. When we directly tell the other what we think, feel, need, or want… surprisingly, our partner most likely responds in a more healthy and direct way. When we communicate in an adult-to-adult manner expressing thoughts and feelings directly, we can then talk to each other's mind and heart for a favorable outcome.

Today I talk to you with respect and use words such as

I think /I want/ I would appreciate _____

and in the future I request that you would_____.

We open our communication in an adult-to-adult fashion, fostering equality and displaying consructive ways to communicate and find win/win solutions .

MARCH 13

Thinking Of You

I love the way you cherish me every day.

I love the way you cherish me each day by calling, leaving notes, or e-mailing me with your latest news and favorite jokes. I hold dear these little daily gestures as they let me know you are thinking of me throughout the day. I feel special and close to you. I hold you next to my heart by saving these priceless thoughts and messages on my telephone, text, or e-mails. Thank you for taking time to think of me. **Today I reciprocate by letting you know that I cherish you by expressing thanks and romantic sentiments through phone messages, notes, texts, or e-mails that you might physically keep as a reminder of your esteemed place in my heart.**

MARCH 14

Pets

Pets demonstrate closeness and unconditional love, which help us to show tenderness.

Oh, the joys pets bring to us! They bring us significant physical comfort by snuggling with us... to get as close as possible to us, and emanating their love in all they do. They have the ability to alleviate emotional and bodily pain with their companionship, loyalty, and affection. Yet amazingly, their needs are simple, wanting only our attention and care for their well-being. Isn't this exactly what we really desire from each other? **Today I show you unconditional love in which you do not need to achieve anything or act a certain way. You are loved for being you..**

MARCH 15

Reading

We are rich in experiences when we read together.

It's such a simple pleasure to have time to just read together, blended as one; being focused on the information and memorable stories that transport us to another world. Sometimes we share stories or excerpts by reading them out loud. These stories have the power to elicit tears and laughter. Other times it keeps us in suspense while waiting for the ending. Reading is more enriching when I do it with you. **Today we take turns reading to each other.**

MARCH 16

Being Myself

I show my truest form of love by being me.

I can show you my deepest love by simply being the person that I am most naturally. This is the purest compliment, because I can trust you so completely. I do not have to hide behind shadows of what I think you want me to be. I feel safe to speak from my heart and act without fear that you may disapprove or become angry. I am truthful with you, because I want you to be your authentic self. **Today I am both spontaneous and consciously aware of being my true self to increase our "into me you see."** I let go of guessing how you might feel or react as my first response. Instead, I know that I can trust you enough to show the genuine me... and that you will reciprocate with being your real self. Then we can be vulnerable enough to be completely intimate.

MARCH 17

New Friends

I am eager to meet your friends.

As you meet new people, I am excited when you invite me to join you in relating to them. When you introduce me to your new friends, I am affirmed you love me and are proud of me. The more I know your friends and acquaintances, the more I glow as they gravitate toward you. You are an incredibly loyal and thoughtful friend and co-worker. I see how your friends are drawn to your humor, wit, honesty, caring, thoughtful, and easy-going nature. You demonstrate your ability to listen and to show compassion to your friends as well as to me. **Today we invite friends over so that we can learn more about them and the ways we interact with others and ourselves.**

MARCH 18

Teamwork

Teamwork draws us closer together.

Whatever we do, I forever appreciate your assistance in working with me. Our tasks may be large or small... they may involve brainstorming strategies and solutions, taking care of our child, washing the dishes, gardening, or shopping even when you would rather be doing something else. I, likewise, am here to aid you when you need help. We are partners in all we do. **Today we discuss ways that we can work together to facilitate chores to build our unity and partnership.**

MARCH 19

Rainy Day

We use rainy days to create a diversion from our routines.

It's so cold, dark, and dreary out... all we want to do is hibernate together and even avoid going outdoors. You frequently coax me out of bed with temptations of a warm, comforting meal—and ask me what I'd like to do. I feel like a child, playing hooky from adult responsibilities, as we plan and scheme to have a fun day indoors. Rain or shine, every day is better with you. **Today we plan or participate in activities for a rainy day, pretending that we're skipping school or work.**

MARCH 20

Walks

Walks are a lesson in nature and beauty.

Ever since we first began walking together, you have taught me about various plants and animals that we encounter. You have often shared your knowledge because you are a keen observer and student... you absolutely love our environment and want to share its beauty with me. You have been a gentle and patient teacher, nurturing my interest in nature through your explanations and demonstrations of our world in motion. I love your teachings, and I want to be your eager student of our natural world. **Today we take a walk and stop to smell the flowers, touch the petals and leaves, observe the wildlife, and to share our knowledge and appreciation of plants and animals that are all around us.**

MARCH 21

Living In The Present

> **By being in the present moment, we are in touch with our feelings, thoughts, and desires.**

Today we commit to living in the present. Moments pass too quickly and it's easy to regret that we were much too worried about the past or future to even fully enjoy the moment. Today... in the here and now, however, we possess the power to influence our fate using our actions to create our future. We let go of the past because we are powerless to change it. Worrying about our future may inhibit and paralyze us... preventing us from ever accomplishing our dreams. We can identify and write down the kind of thoughts that lead to doubt and worry about our past or unsettling events that may happen and change our future. We change these fearful thoughts into those that are soothing and nurturing of ourselves. We think instead of actions that we can take now to lessen and let go of those fears. Today we share these thoughts that limit us and formulate new thoughts that help us to live healthier and more relaxed, productive lives, allowing us to be more confident. If we get stuck, our loved one is there to help listen and ask questions to assist us in clarifying the steps we can take to change our thoughts to those that are more empowering and focused on the present. By making the best choices for our present situation, we are ensuring our best future together.

MARCH 22

Public Affection

We hold hands, hug each other, wrap our arms around each other's waist, and kiss in public.

Affection holds no limits when it comes to our continuing love. Indeed, we are freely uninhibited, whether in private or in the presence of others. When we show each other affection in public, we know it becomes a proclamation of our deep love and bonding. Open affection reflects that we can be ourselves, and that we can truly appreciate and fully enjoy each other's company and the simple pleasure of being together. **Today we proudly proclaim and demonstrate our affection to each other in a public setting.**

MARCH 23

Simple Activities

Any activity with you is special.

Sitting in front of the fire, with the fragrant scent of pines, the flames dancing in various colors and hearing them snap and crackle makes me want to cuddle with you and rest my head on your shoulder. In solitude, we become mesmerized by sitting, listening, and enjoying each other and the simple wonders of nature and our home. You truly light my fire. **Today, we sit in front of the fire or just snuggle together appreciating the quiet and solitude of being alone together.**

51

MARCH 24

Goals

We discuss goals to determine directions for our relationship.

Without goals, we tend to let each day melt one into another, just waiting for something to happen to us. **Today we take turns sharing our dreams of the goals we want to accomplish together in our relationship.** It might be to create a date night each week and what might come of that. It could also be saving for a special vacation, taking a desired class, becoming more physically fit and incorporating healthier eating patterns, or preparing for an event with the other's help and cooperation. Goals help us to stay focused and allow us to set concrete steps to reach them. We discuss our goals, so that we can be united as we encourage each even more.

MARCH 25

Eternity

A lifetime is not enough time to spend with you!

Each day of my life with you is cherished—no matter what we are doing. Each day brings you closer to me as you reveal who you are and show me in so many ways how precious I am to you... and you to me. I never tire of being with you. **Today I take a moment to remind myself the many reasons why I love you and the preciousness of this gift of time. I communicate to you these thoughts and tell you..."a lifetime is not enough time to spend with you!"**

MARCH 26

Pleasuring

I can simply enjoy being touched.

Sometimes we want to be touched in ways that relieve our tension and pain. Other times, we want to be touched in a light, playful way in which we restore our energy and sense of humor. Still, other times we may want to be sexually aroused or pleasured. **Today we draw outlines of our bodies and shade in areas we want to be touched more, disclosing what we each personally desire. Your touch both soothes and lights the fire within.**

MARCH 27

Playfully Romantic

The first time I ever saw your face, I wanted to flirt with you.

Your meaningful looks from across the room signal to me how you cherish me and that you are secure in how much I adore you. Then our eyes meet, sparkling as we smile, and acknowledge the other with perhaps a wink or a tilt of the head. We sense the message behind the dazzling, irresistible smiles that communicate that the sizzle is still there. You are hot! **Today I pretend that you and I are meeting for the first time as I try to pick you up. Will my flirty ways work even now?**

MARCH 28

Sharing

You offer me the first bite of any new or favorite food.

When we go to a restaurant to sample a new dish or entree we both enjoy, you offer me the first bite. I know how hard this is sometimes when you are faced with sharing your favorite dish. Small everyday gestures like this make you even more special to me, because I know how much you care and love me. I notice everything about you. **Today I offer you the first bite of my favorite treat.**

MARCH 29

Our Child

The birth of our child is a gift from God.

Our love and devotion to one another created our child. We eagerly anticipated her birth, and both of us were so ecstatically overwhelmed about how miraculously perfect she was when we first saw her beautiful face and examined her long delicate fingers and toes. We lovingly gazed at every inch of her being with grateful eyes and heart. "Welcome to our world. We've waited so long for you, our beloved daughter. We're eager to share our lives, joy, and love with you." **Today we remember our thoughts, emotions, and what we saw, heard, touched, and felt as we reminisce about the birth of our child.**

MARCH 30

Birth

The birth of our child changes our lives forever.

We tenderly hold our child and bring her home from the hospital. We vow to take care of her eternally, and to nurture and cherish all the elements that transform her from a helpless being to one who feels emotions, thinks independently, and has her own incredible personality and talents. We are eager to teach her what we know and to show her by our actions that we love her unconditionally. We are so blessed to have our daughter in our lives. **We discuss what a child means to us and how we grow together as a family.**

MARCH 31

Giving Attention

When a child is born, we nurture our partners.

When a newborn comes into our lives, we have the tendency to focus most of the attention on that child. Now that our child is here, I want you to know that you are loved and appreciated even more. I realize that we may not have as much time together as before, yet our time together is now even more important. We agree to spend it comforting each other, conversing, working together, relaxing, dining, playing, problem solving, having sexual intimacy, or holding our child, and discussing our dreams for the family. **Today I tell you that you are my chosen one, my lover, my best friend, and my soul mate.** Demonstrating my love to you inspires you to give more love to me and our child.

april

APRIL 1

Laughing

Laughing out loud until tears roll down our faces helps us capture the joys of our lives.

Sometimes we play games with each other. We tell jokes and get the other laughing until our bellies are trembling and aching with pain. At other times we exaggerate and mock the way the other might say things. If we are feeling exuberant, we might jump up and share a "chest bump." We feel like kids again—lighthearted and carefree without any hardships or adult responsibilities. We try to outdo each other, getting vicarious pleasure from seeing how the other laughs uncontrollably, barely able to breathe and eyes becoming teary as we recount a recent event that made us laugh. **Today I want to make you laugh until you have to run to the bathroom!**

APRIL 2

Teamwork

No matter my project or goal, you are there by my side offering assistance.

Your earnest willingness to help with projects and goals that I set for myself touches me. You freely donate your time, energy, and skills to assist me even when you are mired in your own pursuits. I feel and sense that you prioritize me over other people and things. I am truly blessed to have you as my lifelong partner. **Today I help you to define a goal by asking what you want to accomplish, and finding what is it about this goal that makes it so important to you**. I also ask you what actions you can take to achieve your goal and encourage your commitment to them by encouraging you to set behavioral objectives and time deadlines for attaining this. I am fully committed to assisting you by regularly discussing your progress to your goal and encouraging your skills and resources to reach your dreams.

APRIL 3

Friends

You are my best friend, my confidant.

You are without a doubt, my best friend. I want to share my innermost thoughts with you: my happiness, excitement, stress, hurt, sadness, anxiety, anger and hopes. I want to know all about you, and I want you to know the real me, the private me. I reveal my confidences, knowing they are safe within your heart. For you, my love, are my best friend! **Today I share an intimate detail of my thoughts or feelings, and I ask for yours in return.**

APRIL 4

Acts Of Love

I want you to awaken to a sparkling home.

When you go to bed at night, sometimes I look at the disarray in our beautiful home. It may be spoiled by the clutter of paper, dishes, and clothes. While you slumber, I clean our home anticipating your appreciation and delight when you awaken. My energy expands—fueled by thoughts of your love and gratitude. I willingly clean, knowing that this is my labor of love for us both. **Today I willingly and lovingly pick up, clean, or do a household chore to show you my love.**

APRIL 5

Letting Go (Step 1)

I begin to accept and fully love myself to attain the cherishing that I desire.

When we don't allow ourselves to feel precious and cherished, we can't feel valuable or worthy. Instead, we experience shame and a sense of inferiority, as if we are somehow defective. Healing our wounds within ourselves begins by examining the source of our shame—starting the healing process so that we can feel worthy and lovable. We can now begin to understand that we felt different or inadequate as a child. I commit to loving myself by letting go of the shame from my past. These are burdens that I have placed on myself for too long. If I do not overcome my shame, you, my partner, cannot lighten the darkness within my own heart. I can never be satiated enough by your comforting and loving words and actions. Starting with myself—and fulfilling my desire to be loved and cherished, I write and believe in the verbal affirmations I create. **Today I write new thoughts which are stated in the direction I want my behaviors to occur that are focused on desired outcomes.**

♡ I am loveable and worthy.

♡ I accept myself more and more with each passing day.

♡ I let go of shame and awaken miracles in my life.

♡ As I love and accept myself, more opportunities reveal themselves to me.

♡ My relationships become stronger as I value myself.

APRIL 6

Healing (Step 2)

Today I nurture my inner innerchild.

Today I help myself let go of shame, and take a few moments to close my eyes and visualize the first time that I experienced a source of shame when I felt different from others... that somehow I wasn't as good as others. When I am able to focus on the earliest experience that led to feelings of inadequacy and shame, I visualize that scene and determine how old I was in that "picture." I study this image to sense and understand what my inner child was feeling at the time:

- ♡ how old I was,
- ♡ the specific situation, and
- ♡ if there were any other people with me in that scene.

As soon as I answer these questions, I imagine myself going to my inner child at the age when the shame was first evidenced, and I introduce myself as the current-day adult. I let my child know that I am from the future, to assure her that she is going to get through this difficult time. I hug, hold, and talk to my "inner child" in a supportive and loving way—affirming her. When I am ready to leave, I take another look at my younger self and notice that she feels, looks, and sounds different. Yes, step by step, I am healing my mind, emotions and spirit; allowing my inner child to grow.

APRIL 7

Roses

I remember the first time you sent me roses.

When we were apart, I was absolutely thrilled the first time you sent me flowers. I felt your bouquet was possibly the most beautiful arrangement I'd ever received. Caught up in the chivalry of your kind thoughts and actions, I was enraptured by your romantic touch. You displayed all the signs of the man I had been looking for all my life. The sweet fragrance of those roses remains in my mind today. You were and still are the person of my dreams. Thank you for such a wonderful memory of your caring. **Today I tell you how I felt when I first received flowers from you.**

APRIL 8

Affirmations Of Love

Each day I look for what I love and appreciate about you.

As each day emerges, I focus on your actions and warm ways you speak to me. I consciously record those behaviors and your many attributes that I appreciate and admire. And each day, I write down in a special journal or notebook, at least one act of love or something I want to remember about you. By the end of the year, I have wonderful collection of priceless memories and reminders of why I love you so much. **Each day we record an act of love or a thought about the other that fills us with love and appreciation.**

APRIL 9

Reframing

Our perception of an event creates our response.

We hold the ultimate choice to view any situation through various lenses. The one we select, colors the way we feel and respond. Thus, I commit to looking at situations through diverse lenses to determine their meaning and intent to achieve the best results. By acknowledging I have the power to change my thoughts, feelings, and actions, I choose to believe we are doing the very best for you, me, and for our relationship. **Today we experiment and converse about various ways that we can view life situations. We give each other the benefit of the doubt and look for our partner's intentions... and be more accepting of each other's unique differences.**

APRIL 10

Soul Mates

We discuss the moment we both knew we had found our soulmate.

Beginning with our first date, we became lost in our conversations, oblivious of where we were going and focusing only on our words to each other... desperately trying to soaking in all the information our senses could possibly hold. What was our chemistry, the intangibles that drew us together so quickly? **Today we discuss our attractions to each other and that special moment when we began to realize we were truly meant for each other.** You were and still are the most incredibly marvelous and amazing person I have ever met. Thank you for coming into my life and becoming my soulmate.

APRIL 11

Loving Nature

> **I knew by the way you tenderly taught me about nature, that you would be a loving parent.**

I could tell so much about you when you were absorbed in your love of being in nature. The names of the many plants we encountered flowed effortlessly as you explained their various parts and how they worked together. You also described just how each variety was different, and you took care to point out their distinguishing characteristics. I would admire your knowledge of botany, and how you shared the natural world with me. Studying the plants' striking features, you also dug many holes for these new plants to beautify the landscape around our home. You were attentive, carefully watering and fertilizing both the plants and our love so we could grow stronger. **Today we acknowledge our love of nature and the lessons it teaches us, which we can apply to our relationship.**

APRIL 12

Gifting

Whenever I shop, I look for things for you.

Whenever I go to the grocery store or to the mall, I find myself looking for things to purchase for you. Of course, I get a fair share of goods for myself and seem to find wonderful bargains on items that might brighten your day. It could be your favorite food, a bottle of wine, clothes, or something for your hobbies. I eagerly wait for an occasion when I can surprise you with this exceptional gift whether it's a holiday or just an ordinary day. Seeing you smile with delight makes any day remarkable. **Today I have you in the back of my mind as I shop and bring home a gift to brighten your day and show you I care.**

APRIL 13

Discovery

Our love grows stronger with each passing day.

My love for you is limitless. You are my one and only. There are many people on this earth, but no one compares with you. My love, you are my inspiration, the song in my heart. My purpose in life is to continually discover your strengths and uniqueness and share every wondrous moment with you. **I reflect on what I can distinguish about you today.** Is it by observing you? Perhaps I ask you a different question each day about how you consciously show your love towards me. I want to discover the many ways that otherwise might not get noticed or appreciated by me. As we share our thoughts and actions, we are indeed growing our love each day.

APRIL 14

Emotional Support

You are steadfast in being by my side.

When I am stressed or have tough decisions to make, you are there to listen and to provide support. You are so helpful in listening and validating my thoughts and feelings while helping me gain different perspectives. You point out to me the many choices I have. You suggest ways of approaching and handling different people and situations. By role playing with me, at times you've helped me to refine and build confidence in my communication skills. **Today, I give you my full attention and openness to your ideas by listening with all my heart and mind.**

APRIL 15

Sexiness

I put on sexy attire to attract you.

Thank goodness we no longer live in our parents' generation when some mothers slept with big curlers in their hair and gooey cold cream on their faces. How could a man become stimulated with visions of a flannelled cartoon character lying next to him? Likewise, how could a woman become aroused with a man in his dingy t-shirt, frumpy pajamas, and five-o'-clock shadow? We scintillate each other tonight with a feast for our eyes and sensual touches. Perhaps a silk gown for me and silky pajama bottoms for you... or do we dare reveal even more? You'll have to find out tonight! **Tonight we put on seductive attire for each other to enhance our visual pleasures and arouse the passion witiin.**

APRIL 16

Embracing

Holding the other when we drift off to sleep ensures sweet dreams.

How deliciously loved I feel as you embrace me when I come to bed. You continue to hold me until your breath changes; a change signaling peacefulness and quiet slumber. **I can feel safe and protected in your arms, knowing you are there for me even in your unconscious moments.** This symbolizes love in the purest form.

APRIL 17

Anger

When feelings of anger and irritation arise I commit to talking to you right away.

On occasions, we have allowed our anger to temporarily cause emotional and physical distance between us. Especially early in our relationship, I did not have the courage to tell you how I felt. Instead, I mistakenly held my feelings in until I exploded over a minor incident. Each and every day I share my angry feelings with you as they come up. I do so lovingly, to resolve our problems and strengthen our love. We commit to sharing irritations as we become aware of them. By our promises and behaviors, we are building emotional intimacy and being proactive in being transparent to solve dilemmas together. Honest communication is the first step in our preserving and honoring our love for each other. **Today we commit to talking together as soon as feelings of anger arise as a way of keeping our emotions manageable and productive.**

APRIL 18

Family Fun

Our marriage is enriched by family activities.

One of our favorite activities is to bowl together. We cheer each other on, whether it is a thrilling strike or a perhaps a disappointing gutter ball. The game often becomes joyfully punctuated with bursts of loud approval when the pins fall down and excited reassurances when they don't. Our efforts are rewarded by the splintering of the pins falling down. We dance, smile and laugh together as we share this fun activity. **Today we pick a physical activity that gets our bodies moving and sharing a happy family time.**

APRIL 19

Born To Be Wild

The wind in our hair brings out the animal in us.

We take a ride in a convertible, a truck, or car with the windows rolled down. The joy we share begins with feeling the wind sweep through our tussled hair... engulfed in a convergence of air, with the music blaring as the highway stretches before us. We feel so free, seemingly so powerful and alive. We feel the car vibrating effortlessly as the rubber meets the road. We are one with the music and the wind transporting us to another time and place. **Today we take a ride on the wild side heading into the sunset.**

APRIL 20

Physical Touch

Sometimes, the way to listen is through touch.

When we want the other to listen, sometimes it is our nonverbal touch which speaks the loudest. When we feel troubled, we may not want to talk. Yet when we first take the time to reconnect with each other by touching, whether it's a caress, a kiss, holding hands, or rubbing each other's backs, we can immediately feel a transfer of tenderness. Our trust is restored as our guard comes down, enhancing the possibility of better understandings. **Today we touch to fully listen and support.**

APRIL 21

Resentments

I let go of old resentments and start anew.

Today I choose to let go of old, angry feelings from the past. Anger has made me impatient and critical of you—the one I love the most. Instead, I now focus on what I can do to forgive you and give myself permission to heal my own anger. The start of forgiving you might be through prayer, in which I release my anger and bless you. The next step might be as simple as recognizing your love for me. I remind myself that I am taking your action personally when it has nothing to do with me. Still another way is to examine what it is about me that can cause so much anguish. Can I learn a lesson from this to grow even healthier? Forgiving you is an act of love for both you and me.

APRIL 22

Friday Evenings

Friday at sunset signals for us to put our work aside and enjoy family time.

Friday at sunset signals the end of the work week and the beginning of rest. This ritual calls for family unity where we enjoy a peaceful meal, talk, and relax. Going so fast throughout the week, we frequently lose connection to the ones who are closest to us. Each Friday, we look forward to initiating the "evening of rest," to revitalize our family love and to recharge our batteries as we look forward to the weekend ahead. No work and no worries on Friday evenings!

APRIL 23

Intimacy

The more intimate I am with you, the closer you move towards me.

Intimacy is the ability to freely give and receive affection and to be so trusting of you that I can be myself. I trust you completely because you accept me so unconditionally. In turn, I reveal to you more of who I am. You join me in the dance, by sharing your most personal sentiments and secrets. When you revealed that I might feel disappointed in you, I had an opportunity to clarify and affirm that you have been exactly the opposite... surpassing all my expectations for a partner who has achieved so much in our marriage and in your life. We allow ourselves to be vulnerable and are anointed with an incredible friendship and soulful bond. **Today we share an intimate detail that our partner may not know.**

APRIL 24

Wisdom

I am empowered to change myself, not you.

I saw the gem in you when we met. As time passed, I began to think that you would be even better if you made certain changes. I then tried to change you, sometimes subtly, manipulating in a gentle way, to let you think this was your idea. Other times my attempts to change you were abrupt and demanding. Both efforts resulted in your refusal to change. However, all was not lost. You began to change once you saw a change in my response. When I revealed my emotions and directly requested you to change certain behaviors, you understood the reasons behind my wants and needs. You then changed because you understood what I needed and why. We became steadfast partners—teamed together to build our relationship. When I have the urge to change you, I examine my own needs and motivation. How does this help me, you, or us? **Today we start with changes within ourselves—conducting an honest personal inventory, and seeking to better assess both our strengths and weaknesses**. By discussing these assessments, we begin to understand how our characteristics and behaviors can impact ourselves and each other.

71

APRIL 25

Interests

Whatever is my newest interest, I want to share it with you.

Because we continue to evolve as individuals, our synergistic lives become richer. Stemming from change, we also develop new interests and hobbies, **Today we promise to introduce the other to any new interests which may occur.** I am eager to introduce new activities to you, my love. Everything is more fun, fuller, and exciting when we share activities together. By participating in the other's interests, we show our love.

APRIL 26

A Quick Massage

While working or relaxing, you massage my neck and shoulders.

Aaah! The areas where I carry my stress and tension are in my neck and shoulders. Whenever I am deluged with information and pressures, you seem to intuitively sense my growing overload. My neck, my shoulders, and my body all thank you when you start working your magic fingers—kneading and stroking, alternating the tempo of slow and brisk movements, touching both softly and firmly. Will you take a kiss and a hug as payment? **Today I reward your efforts by giving you a massage.**

APRIL 27

Jokes

You enliven my day with your jokes.

Almost daily, you tell or send me jokes, providing the relief I need. I am delighted when I receive them as they lighten and brighten my day. I smile and laugh, and I can't stop thinking about you. On one lively road trip we read jokes out loud in the car during the entire journey. Traveling has never gone faster or was more packed with laughter. **Today we tell some jokes to each other until we laugh out loud**

APRIL 28

Vacations

Let's go on a vacation and "hang loose."

Too often we get caught up in the strains of daily life with its heavy financial burdens and our frenetic pace. **Today we discuss and create a getaway plan to energize us with anticipation for the future.** This can be a simple overnight trip to the mountains or a local resort, or it can be more elaborate with a longer vacation. We excitedly await the start of adventure, wonder, anticipation, and the seduction of good times ahead. Relaxation, fun, and new discoveries are the perfect remedy to soothe our fragile, frazzled lives. Let's go!

APRIL 29

Supporting and Nurturing

I want to be the first to support, encourage, and nurture you and the last to criticize.

I want to be your primary and greatest supporter in everything you choose to do... whether it involves hobbies, interactions with others, work, or personal pursuits. **Today I am at your side to offer comfort, to discuss ideas, or to verbally and physically show you that I care.** I totally and completely believe in you. I want you to realize that I don't want to be critical, my dearest. If I do sound critical, please tell me directly that what I say has hurt you. I promise I will listen.

APRIL 30

Volunteering

By focusing on the needs of others in our community through volunteering, we share our gifts and are grateful.

We feel gratified when we volunteer together for community service by helping to build or repair homes, picking up trash, or distributing much needed clothes and toys, and reading to children. In helping our city, we also help ourselves, as we experience gratitude for all the wonderful blessings we have. It seems the more we give, the more we receive in return. When we share we are rewarded with feelings of gratitude and the knowledge we make a postiive difference. **Today we do an act of kindness for our community.**

may

MAY 1

Sending Flowers

Receiving plants and flowers at our home or office causes my heart to skip a beat.

When you send plants and flowers to my workplace or to our home, I am overjoyed by your generous and thoughtful gestures. I excitedly call you and thank you profusely. I pause to lovingly admire the arrangement and send telepathic messages of love to you throughout the day. Have you received those heartfelt messages of love and gratitude? You are the best! **Today I send you a gift and imagine your smile**.

MAY 2

Happily In Love

> We know we're madly in love when we want the whole world to know about each other.

Whomever I meet, if I converse with them long enough, learns of you. Even casual acquaintances hold no doubt about my adoration for you. When I talk about you, others can see the sparkle in my eyes, the smile on my face, and the animation in my voice as I enthusiastically describe your virtues. I want the world to know about you and our unbelievable out-of-this-world relationship! **Today I tell at least one person what I love about you or the gratitude I hold in my heart for you.**

MAY 3

Viewing Photographs

Examining your journey through childhood, youth, and into adulthood through photographs helps me appreciate the capable, mature, generous, and loving person you've become.

We retrieve our photo albums; what fun looking at pictures from your early years. Your face is filled with mischief and you are pudgy, but oh, so cute! Seeing you a few years later, your lean body is sturdy and your eyes and smile are so full of vitality. Each photo is unforgettable and mesmerizing. I never tire of seeing these fresh-faced images of your youth as these priceless images document the distance you have come on your journey. I can see the changes which make you more remarkable. I love the person that you have become, even though that mischievous look still remains. **Today we look at photos together from our childhood to appreciate and admire the qualities of our past which contribute to the persons we each have become.**

77

MAY 4

Meeting For Lunch

Meeting you for lunch at one of our favorite restaurants brightens my day.

We naturally look forward to meeting for lunch, even if it's just for an hour. The pure enjoyment of eating delicious food, relaxing together, and sharing how our day is going is sheer indulgence. **Today I set a time to have lunch with you, my favorite date, so we can share our day and our bites of food.**

MAY 5

Trust And Vulnerability

Even in my most private moments, I invite you in.

Rarely have we witnessed the other crying. However, it is when we have experienced times of sorrow or pain, we approach each other with extreme care and tenderness, offering an invitation to hold hands, receive a back rub, or simply to embrace. Our compassion and empathy for one other strengthens even more as our deepest love, trust, and emotions are exposed. We are safe with each other. **Today we think of a very private moment when we have expressed our deepest fears and vulnerabilities.** We discuss how it felt to disclose to the other, and how the other responded in thoughts, feelings, actions, and sensations. Did we feel honored to have that information shared to with us? Did we feel so much closer? How did it feel for us to soothe and comfort our partner?

MAY 6

Pleasuring Each Other

I let you know through touch and words how I'd like you to stimulate me. Sex is not an act, but a series of loving gestures in which we take turns pleasuring the other by

I want you completely.

caressing and touching—both slowly and quickly, lightly or firmly, and finding the right cadence and rhythm until we are joined as one, moving as one, and mirroring the other. ***Today we show and tell each other how we can bring out even more passion and pleasure... and I want you to go first!***

MAY 7

Generosity

Especially when finances are tight, I appreciate even more how generous you are with me.

I resisted going to a seminar, saying it was too costly. Yet you persisted, wanting me to have opportunities to maximize quality time with peers and advance my career. You were concerned about my driving back and forth to this conference. You persuaded me to stay at the site of the meetings, believing my safety was worth any cost. When you are altruistic and are focused on my comfort, safety, and ease, I appreciate how charitable and giving you are. ***Today we think of a time we were generous with the other and re-enact a giving behavior.***

MAY 8

Whispering

You whisper "sweet nothings" into my ear that mean everything to me.

You tease me with your breath… tickling my ears and neck. You whisper endearing names and profess your love, quickening my pulse. As the years pass, these gestures mean even more to me, making our love all the more remarkable and vibrant, mainly because we consciously choose to affirm the other with touch and words. We can easily become distracted and preoccupied with our own needs and comfort. You are too dear to ever be taken for granted. **I show you even more the extent of my uncontained love by whispering "sweet somethings" in your ear.**

MAY 9

The Bedroom

Our bed is a sacred place for intimate conversations, sleeping, and making love.

When we disagree and our tempers start to flare, we do not continue our fighting in bed. Instead we may go for a walk or talk in a public place. Some of our best arguments have occured in small restaurants, where we carefully choose our words and modulate our tone to air our thoughts and feelings. We are aware our anger does not serve us well; instead our anger briefly rules us. It is during these occasions that we take a "time out" to restore calmness. Only when emotions are controlled can we discuss volatile topics. **All potentially explosive subjects are off limits from our bed which is a place of safety, love, and rest. Instead, we pledge from now on to air our differences before we go to bed.**

MAY 10

Passion

After all these years, my passion for you is still fresh.

We are an amazing testament to the fact that the longer we are together, the more we grow even ever closer. Our love is still fresh. You are the one that excites me. You are the one I want to be with. You are the one that quickens my heart and takes my breath away. You are the one I rush home to at night! You are the one that lightens my day, fills my heart with joy, and revitalizes me. **Today we ignite our passion with a surprise gesture of love as we eagerly rush home.**

MAY 11

Loving While Disagreeing

The next time we argue, we hold hands and look into each other's eyes.

We resolve the next time we have a disagreement, we hold hands and look into the other's eyes. It's hard to stay angry or to raise our voices when we are physically linked. We talk softly, directly, and constructively. By taking turns and using "I statements" to describe our perception, we learn how we are affected by the other's actions and words. I am better able to understand you through looking and touching. How can I stay angry when I feel your energy vibrating through my body and looking at your eyes, clearly giving clues to resolving the hurt and disappointment inside!

MAY 12

Acknowledging And Sharing Chores

Seeing our shower glass sparkle reminds us of how we work together in all we do.

I cherish how you frequently compliment me about how our shower looks brand new because of my diligence in using the squeegee to dry it each time I use it. I also appreciate each and every thoughtful remark and similarly compliment you when you do the same thing. We share household duties equally knowing relationships thrive best when we balance work, play, and other activities. Starting the day with a compliment brings a smile to my face and rapture to my heart. **Today we acknowledge the other's hard work and effort.**

MAY 13

Create The "Setting"

Establishing a romantic setting is all about the context.

We often talk about setting the table. Yet the most important thing for us to remember as a couple is that we can choose to create a mood of romance and relaxation… utilizing conscious, thoughtful actions. You choose soothing music to accompany dinner. You dim the lights to provide a sense of tranquility which helps transition from work to an evening of relaxation in our home. Eating dinner by candle light is romantic and creates a special bond for us and our family. **Today we create a mood we'd like to enjoy more whether it is simply more calming, romantic, energizing, or playful and fun for the family.**

MAY 14

Staying Healthy

I want you to be with me forever.

I want you to take the very best care of yourself. If I am critical about what you eat or drink, please understand it is because I love you so much. I want us to always be together. I am selfish, and I want you to do everything possible to promote your health and your emotional and spiritual well-being. In return, I pledge that I will take the very best care of my body, mind, and spirit. **We commit our efforts to eat healthier and more nutritious meals at home. Together we plan and select menus which are appealing to us both**.

MAY 15

Supporting

Today I support your efforts in whatever you do.

At times I haven't supported you—your feelings, thoughts, actions, or dreams. I know how disappointed you have been when I fail to be there 100% for you. I apologize for my actions. **Today I listen, encourage, praise, and respect you without judgment. I let go of what I think you should do and acknowledge you are the expert of your life.**

MAY 16

Stroking Your Hair

I want to use my senses to fully experience you.

When I brush or softly stroke your hair, I become caught in the rhythm of the movement, noticing my wrist and arms smoothly and gently moving back and forth. I savor the smell and texture of your skin. I know I can give you moments of pleasure by just being with you and sharing a loving touch. Simple comforts such as brushing your hair can produce such closeness for us. **Today we take turns using our senses to fully experience the other**.

MAY 17

Making Affirmations

Verbal affirmations from you brighten my day!

The power of magic can happen when we use affirmations to positively acknowledge, and also validate, the values we see in each other. It is a delightful and loving way of showing our appreciation. Simple phrases such as "thank you for..." and "I love the way you..." remain forever etched in my memory. They remind me how loved I am by you, and how I assist you in making our life's journey a little easier. Your affirmations softly urge me to fall in love over and over again. **Today I recognize and acknowledge an action or attribute about you and what this means to me.**

MAY 18

Enjoying Nature

Being one in nature restores us.

When we needed to recharge our energies and rejuvenate our spirits, we have often turned to nature. Hiking a mountain trail, napping on a beach, or fishing along a stream are all ways we can experience the wonderment and peace of nature. It is so magical being quiet and alive in nature. **Today we go back to nature to be restored physically and emotionally. We are in touch with the beauty around us. We are embraced by the serenity and strength of nature.**

MAY 19

Growing

Growing and nurturing love has helped me to grow as a person.

Like a plant that has been tenderly placed in the ground, fertilized, and watered, which then blossoms into fragrant flowers and sturdy stalks of leaves, your love has helped me to transcend from ordinary to extraordinary. Your love has helped me to be the person that I have always wanted to be—by your encouragement to speak my mind, to take actions, and to evolve into someone I'm happy to be—I am proud, confident, self-assured, joyful, optimistic, and caring because of your nurturing. You allowed me to take steps to find myself, to be the genuine me by continually accepting me for the person who I am. For that I will continually be grateful and love you. **Today I encourage you to grow and be your true self by voicing words of love and acceptance.**

MAY 20

Rebirthing

We gratefully and lovingly express what our child means to us.

So often we become embroiled in our daily parenting routines of disciplining, helping with homework, and struggling to maintain loving relations with our children. **Today we choose to "recreate" the birth of our child, wanting to recapture all the "first love", gratefulness, preciousness, ecstasy, and relief following her birth.** We felt these emotions when she was born and express them now so she can feel and understand our love and elation. "We welcome you with open arms and hearts. We are so happy you are our daughter. You are perfect exactly the way you are. We cherish you, adore you, and want to show how much we love you each and every day. You are our gift from God." We say these loving words along with caressing and holding our child. Even when our daughter was too young to understand the exact words, she completely understood our intentions and feelings. Yes, we love you in every way!

MAY 21

Praying

Each night I go to bed and say a prayer.

Each night before I drift off to sleep, I close my eyes and say a prayer for you. I ask God to keep you healthy and safe, to help guide you in His footsteps, to assist you in your career, and thank Him for our love, our marriage, and the wonders of our lives. I know that you pray for me as well. We are indeed blessed to have God's tender love and grace, our love, our health, our child, and the gift of each other. **Today we send positive intentions and energies to all those whom we care about through prayer.**

MAY 22

Bike Rides

Bike rides together as a couple, or with our family, promote fun and closeness.

Riding our bikes can be an adventure, encouraging us to exercise, to breathe fresh air, and to be fully absorbed in the environment surrounding us. As we inhale deeply, buoyed by our senses, our muscles flex as we pedal, varying our efforts to match the difficulty of the terrain. We pace each other to reach our destination where a tasty breakfast or an ice cold smoothie is consumed. This brief rest allows us to converse about what we saw and experienced. Pedaling home, we feel a sense of accomplishment and communality of purpose. That was fun, let's do it again! **Today we ride a bike or engage in a physical activity that lets us enjoy the freshness and inspiration of being outdoors.**

MAY 23

Making Friends

Our friends become our "family of choice."

We seem to easily attract people to us, some who could become good friends. We carefully choose our trusted allies among these friends. They become our "family of choice." These, our closest friends, share our joys and pains, and entrust us with their confidences. In turn, they extend their support and love to us unconditionally. We rejoice knowing we have a group of loyal friends, who are also our extended family. **Today we take time to appreciate and rejoice in our "family of choice."**

MAY 24

Managing Sex In Relationships

Occasionally, loving you means sexual intimacy when I'm not in the mood.

Not every sexual moment is preceded by candlelight dinners and lengthy body massages. Your tender sexual needs are important to me. I want you to feel satisfied and fulfilled, and content with me as a loving partner. At times our sexual needs may not be in synch. I choose to be sexually present with you and want to help you be emotionally and physically satisfied. I want you to be there for me, too, knowing that we both can pleasure the other. Sometimes these sexual interludes are like appetizers for later in the week. **Today I remind myself giving you sexual pleasure is one way I show my love.**

MAY 25

Taking Breaks

> **No matter how busy you are, you make time for me.**

Sometimes you are so busy. Yet you stop when I ask you for your time. You give me your undivided attention in the midst of your many tasks and unfailingly give me that look and smile which says "I'm glad you interrupted me." Even when you're fighting time pressures, you stop briefly and promise to talk or engage in activities with me at your earliest opportunity. You give me loving assurance in acknowledging my needs and show me how you prioritize your time with me. **I commit to doing the same for you, so that even if I'm harried and hurried; I show you today and every day that I value you by giving you my undivided attention when you ask for it.**

MAY 26

Conflicts

Conflicts give us information so that we can improve our relationship with each other.

Whenever our relationship is going smoothly and we feel connected, it is often the best time for us to discuss the conflicts we experience in our relationship. When our emotions are calmer, we are able to think clearer and be less judgmental and critical of each other. We are then able to choose our words much more carefully as we better modulate our voices to enable our ideas and feelings to be better accepted by the other. It is during these times, that I can appreciate your earnestness for positive changes rather than viewing your communication as "picking a fight" with me. **Today we examine issues in our relationship that prevent us from having the love that we both desire, and we set a time and place to begin discussing these.**

MAY 27

Letting Go

Real love is letting go to allow you to follow your dreams.

True love is allowing you to be yourself rather than the person you think I want you to be. I don't define you. You define yourself. I want you to be able to express who you are in any way you desire. It may be verbal, nonverbal, artistic, or simply creating your own space. I want you to have time alone to find yourself because I love you so much. Go ahead and be free to explore the possibilities you desire. **Today I give you your own personal space to focus on your needs and goals.**

MAY 28

Telephone Conversations

Remember the days when we'd call each other and breathe heavily into each other's ears?

What fun we had teasing each other by sharing exaggerated breathlessness, instantly heating the room—and our romance. We could be so frivolous and naughty. We loved to hear the other giggle, making it even more enticing when we called at the other's place of work. Unfortunately, we have changed over the years. We've become so politically correct. **Just for today we go back to our silly ways for old time's sake. We tease each other on the telephone and wait for the laugher to erupt.**

MAY 29

Little Gestures

Your appreciation makes me glow inside.

One day on my way to work, the traffic was badly backed up. I called to warn you of the situation so you could take another route to get to work on time. You were so grateful. Your appreciation was evident in your sweet voice, thanking me for my call. Despite my own concern about getting to work on time, I was able to make it through the traffic jam with a smile on my face because of your words. **Today I am reminded of how much you care for me by letting your gratitude bolster me during the difficult commute.** When I struggle with other problems in the future, I think of how you have been there for me. I know that whatever difficulties I may face will be bearable due to your love and support.

MAY 30

Being Roosters And Night Owls

We make common time together.

Sometimes we seem to be opposites. You nod off to sleep so easily in the evenings while I start to come alive at dusk, walking like a vampire in the wee hours of the mornings. Yet, somehow we manage to have enough time together, because we pack in as much activity as possible in those communal hours. **Today I go to bed earlier to be with you. Will you stay up later with me tomorrow?**

MAY 31

Recognizing Uniqueness

No one in the world is like you.

You are like a beautiful snowflake that has been infused with good intentions. As each snowflake is unique and awe-inspiring—so are you. I find you to be the most wonderful person in the world to me. Continually, I am uplifted by your love. Your qualities of tenderness, talent, wit, wisdom, and powerful energy amaze me. You create vigor and life in me. In the entire world, there is no other like you! **Today we express to our partner, "Indeed there is no one like you!"**

june

JUNE 1

Compromising

We create win-win situations.

In our relationship, it's not your way or my way. We are both vitally strong and determined people. We freely voice our opinions yet we listen to each other's needs and wants. We may disagree; we are mindful that we want to be true partners. In healthy relationships, we realize there is no winner or loser. Rather, we both give to attain what we want... and we both end up winners. Otherwise, over time, resentment begins to evolve and derail us. We keep our focus on the goal of what we want to achieve for us. **Today we create a compromise by discussing what we each want, and meeting in the middle. We are both winners and feeling closer.**

JUNE 2

Nurturing Health

If I could give you a gift, it would be the gift of health.

I wish that I had the power to heal your physical maladies. Yet, I watch helplessly as you take your pills, or apply salve to heal your wounds. Although you are in physical pain at times, this does not prevent you from asking me how I'm feeling or flashing that award-winning smile of yours. May my love soothe and help make your days better. **I help you monitor your health. I am pleased to assist in taking care of you**. When you are in pain or not feeling well, I want to be even more tender with you physically and emotionally. I might ask if you would like a cold refreshing juice or a cool or hot gel application. Perhaps it is simply touching and massaging the aching area. Please... always know I am here to comfort you in every way possible, today and all days.

JUNE 3

Resolving Differences

Because I love you so deeply, I may also feel the greatest sadness with you.

My emotions appear to reach their greatest magnitude when I am with you. You often help me to experience my most magnificent highs. I have also experienced devastating lows when we have quarreled or you have said something that attacked my core. **Today I commit to talking with you about your behaviors, not your character, when I am hurt or angry with you.** Let's experience our highest form of love by revealing a time when we felt saddened or hurt by the other's comment or action. We have a chance to learn from the past and heal those old wounds by listening and affirming each other now. In this manner, we experience a greater level of intimacy and love.

JUNE 4

Apologies

I want to be the first to apologize when I am in error.

When I apologize, I want you to realize that my sorrow is sincere. I do not apologize simply to get our relationship back to a more natural and comfortable level. Instead, my heart is heavy, and I want to assume responsibility for my actions. When we blame each other, we harm our relationship. **Today I spend a moment to consider if I have hurt or upset you in some way.** Taking responsibility, and making amends by fully apologizing for specific statements and behaviors that may have angered, disappointed, saddened, or hurt you, help us to let go and start anew.

I am truly sorry I said or did _____.

I sense that you might have felt _____.

Please forgive me for _____.

JUNE 5

Getting It Done

The universe rewards action being taken.

We learned long ago that nothing really just "comes" to us. Rather, we are responsible for creating our lives, our own happiness, and our love. We cannot just ponder what we want because that does not bring us closer to the results that we seek. Instead, we must take steps to achieve what we truly desire. **Today we determine the actions we want to take.** We create a plan and work together to bring it to fruition—by committing to two or three steps we undertake, in setting deadlines to accomplish these actions. We celebrate our commitment with hugs and kisses!

JUNE 6

Self-Examining

When I find myself becoming critical of you, I examine what is making me unhappy.

There are times when I find myself short or impatient with you. During those times, it is easy for me to look at you with a critical eye. Yet these are the very times I want to stop and identify exactly what is going on inside of me that is not quite right. What is causing me to be unhappy, angry, or frustrated? Is it really about you—or is it about me? Once I discover the deeper reason for my thoughts and feelings, I communicate these reasons and needs to you. I appreciate your understanding nature. **Today I go within myself to examine the cause of my frustration and irritation, to determine if I am really unhappy with something in myself.**

JUNE 7

Pride

I am so proud of who you are and who you have become.

You realized at a young age, the most important thing was to respect yourself and know that a strong character is essential. I am aware that you have learned to be honest, open, strong, gentle, and tender. In addition, you are an impressive and articulate communicator. Your qualities of being honorable, loving, and nurturing have guided you along this path. I am so proud to say you are my mate and the person I admire more than anyone else. **Today I explain why I am proud of you.**

JUNE 8

Moments Of Appreciation

I still marvel at our surroundings every time I enter our home.

At night when everyone has gone to bed, I take time to enjoy the beautiful views and replenish myself in the tranquility of our home. I think of how hard we have worked to make our dream home a reality. When I come to bed feeling so grateful, I feel even closer to you. I nestle next to you, feeling our love even when we sleep. Thank you for our beautiful home, family, and marriage. **Today before we go to bed, we stop to admire our home and environment and reflect on how fortunate we are.**

JUNE 9

Doing Things Together

You willingly choose an activity that brings joy and excitement to me.

Sometimes we spend each day of our limited vacation playing golf. That's pretty remarkable knowing your distaste for the game and how easy it would be for you to just give it up. Yet there you are, my partner, willingly by my side taking your shots, and maybe a few mulligans too. Now that's true love... immersing yourself in an activity which is not, nor ever will be, your favorite. This is one way of showing just how much you love me. And I, in turn, willingly water and cultivate our plants, knowing how much this means to you to enrich our yard. **Today we each do an activity which the other prefers to show the depth of our love.**

JUNE 10

Circle Of Love

A perfect circle of love begins by placing one hand over the other's heart—while we join hands.

Today we take the time to place our hands over each other's hearts as we join hands. In the silence of the room, I can hear and feel the fluttering of your heart. I also detect the slight movement of your chest slowly moving up and down...gently, rhythmically and methodically. I notice that my breathing begins to mimic yours, our bodies in perfect harmony. We mirror the other, feeling at once calm, serene, and united. My heart is in your hands.

JUNE 11

Thoughtfulness

You ask me if I need a drink.

You consistently ask me if I would like something to eat or drink whenever you go into the kitchen. Your kindness and considerate gesture affirms your love to me multiple times each day. How much do I love you? Let me count the ways. Each day you reinforce our love through simple acts of kindness like this. **Today we do a thoughtful act for each other to nourish our love.**

JUNE 12

Reminiscing

Reminiscing about our favorite dates helps us to recapture excitement, joy, and passion.

Remember how we jumped into each other's arms when we first saw each other? We even performed parodies of lovers running in slow motion toward the other. We were so consumed with mirth that we couldn't wait to be together. **Today we remember and talk about those special times that passed all too quickly, yet forever remain in our memories. Today we speak with one another about recapturing those feelings of innocence amid the passion of our frisky pastimes.**

JUNE 13

Acknowledging

You are quick to acknowledge my efforts when I do something to please you.

Today I chose a movie for us to attend. It wasn't one that you had considered, but you willingly went along with my suggestion. As soon as the show ends, you softly compliment me on my recommendation. No wonder I can be myself in expressing my thoughts and desires. I appreciate your gesture and take time to thank you for noticing and acknowledging my choices at times when they are different from yours. Thank you for your love. **I commit to immediately recognize your effort and show my appreciation ... as soon as I notice a gesture which pleases me.**

JUNE 14

Eating Out

We sit close to each other at a restaurant.

Today as we wait for our food to arrive, we sit next to each other, with our bodies leaning into each other to close the space. We look attentively at each other while we speak. All the noise from the surrounding patrons fades into the background with only your presence reaching my consciousness. Our conversations transcend what we did today, we also speak of dreams, gratitude, and struggles in our lives—building our love and intimacy.

JUNE 15

Freedom

We have the ability to choose the way we view the world.

Our private perceptions impact everything… they influence the way we might think, feel, and respond. **Today we take the time to examine alternative ways of looking at how we think.** We may view what is happening to us and the way someone else has responded to us differently. Do we want to change our attitudes? Our ability to reinterpret or reframe situations allows us to be calmer, less angry, and more open to the ways we interpret the actions of our partner and others. By being more consciously loving and less judgmental of ourselves and those with whom we come into contact, we become freer. Now we are able to choose interactions and bond with the people most important to us, attributing positive intentions and motives as we give others the benefit of their thoughts and deeds.

JUNE 16

Loving Massage

After a long day, you indulge me with a loving neck massage.

Neck massages can be long or short, and they can be given anywhere. These brief physical connections are welcomed and appreciated! There are times when you provide me with your loving strokes while I'm standing by the stove preparing dinner. At other times, I receive this treat tender touch while sitting on the sofa or lying in bed. Whenever, and whatever the occasion, I readily welcome your pampering touch. Thank you, my love, for making the end of my day so relaxing. **Today we offer the other the soothing gift of touch.**

JUNE 17

Trust

I give you my heart to hold forever with my pledge of love and devotion to you.

Whenever I am with the opposite sex in a work or social setting, I am aware of and maintain healthy physical and emotional boundaries. I highly honor and prioritize your closeness to me. Because I honor your closeness to me, I am fully faithful to you and trust your devotion completely. Sometimes out of necessity we separately have meetings, dinners, or engage in activities with other men and women who share common interests. We both know we have the other's complete trust to respect the boundaries of work and friendship. I appreciate your trust in me and feel confident of your fidelity to me. **Today and every day, I am secure in trusting you when you are with others, which further encourages you to share your experiences with me.**

JUNE 18

Sending Greeting Cards

Today I send you a card especially for being you.

In this entire world, there is only one you. **Today I keep our love fresh simply by sending romantic cards to remind you of how special you are to me.** The world is a better place, because you are in it. I want you to know how much I love and cherish you for simply being you. When I receive these cards as a surprise, they are appreciated even more. I read the sentiments knowing they are prompted by your heart rather than by something that is expected of you. May this greeting card lift your heart today as a gift showing my love for you.

JUNE 19

Parents

Spending time with your parents gives me a glimpse into your past.

When we are with our parents we are sometimes transported back to our youth. When we can engage your parents in sharing aspects of your past, I frequently use these valued interactions to further my understanding of just how you have become the marvelous person that you are. You have taken the best parts of your family to become healthy and caring, having learned to treat each person with equality, integrity, and respect. **Today we spend time with your parents, and show them our appreciation for contributing to the adult you are today.**

JUNE 20

Changing Family Rules And Beliefs

We have become healthy, loving adults by consciously developing our own personal identity and beliefs rather than automatically endorsing the established beliefs which may no longer be beneficial to retain. These old beliefs may have even been some

> **We examine our rules and beliefs to determine if they are healthy and adaptive.**

passed on through generations. **Today, we write down the old beliefs we were raised with and examine each to determine whether we want to keep these rules or beliefs, or to modify them.** We may also create brand new rules for thinking and acting which ensure us greater happiness and balance to enhance our present and future. For instance, we might have been told or learned it's wrong to show or express anger which leads us to suppress that emotion. Instead we might develop a different belief, for example, that anger is just another emotion, which can be freely expressed in nourishing, respectful, and assertive ways by describing perceptions and actions contributing to anger. By adopting this new belief about anger providing helpful information to us, we are freer to express as these emotions arise.

JUNE 21

Gifting

I willingly give you the gift of my love

It's so easy to give you a gift signifying my love. At times that "gift" may be simply cooking your favorite meal, presenting you with a clean house, buying you something that I know will bring you pleasure, or it might be a handwritten list of what I love about you, which is proudly displayed in our home... or simply giving you kisses from your head to your toes. Gifts cost nothing with a little time and imagination, yet can mean so much to us when given with love. **Today I give you a gift as a token of my affection**.

JUNE 22

Forgiving

The ultimate form of love is to forgive another.

We are no longer satisfied with "resolving" our differences. We want to let go of our past anger and hurts and to be able to start afresh. We follow an ancient Hawaiian ritual called Ho'oponopono to cleanse and to create a new beginning of warmth and compassion for both of us. As we look into each other's eyes, we hold hands, and take turns saying the following twice:

♡ I'm sorry

♡ Please forgive me

♡ Thank you

♡ I love you

Whenever we are ready to let go and forgive, we leave our pain, regrets, and sorrow behind as we practice the symbolic ritual of Ho'oponopono.

JUNE 23

Fantasizing

We playfully imagine that we're on a deserted island.

We create the adrenline rush of adventure! Should we go to the beach and pretend that we washed up on the shore? Can we use our wits to locate water, food, and shelter? How do we team together to thrive in a new environment, or do we go for the other's throat? Only you and I have the storyline for our adventure! It's another cliff hanger! We are again in our youth—playfully recreating a type of Swiss Family Robinson or being in the wilderness as pioneers. What type of games can we create? Do we try new foods? **Today, we create ideas and scripts for our adventurous discoveries.**

JUNE 24

Creating Time Together

We prioritize and examine ways to increase time together.

Without adequate time together, it is easy to become lost in the everyday shuffle of routine tasks and actions. We affirm the importance to develop other ways we can spend precious time with one another. Perhaps it involves getting up 15 minutes earlier to share breakfast or going to bed 15 minutes earlier at night to have "quiet time." We might consider carpooling with each other to gain extra time to talk, or even using the commuting time to reconnect and prepare for developments at home. You are an important priority. I set aside time for you each day. **Today we discuss and commit to setting aside at least 15 minutes each day to give each other undivided attention.**

JUNE 25

Embracing Family And Friends

We welcome our family and friends into our lives.

I welcomed your parents with open arms when we married. I wanted an extension of my own family that I could get to know and love. You cherished my family because they produced me. Likewise, your family and friends are very important to me. These friendships demonstrate your attractiveness to others who value the same qualities I so admire and love in you. Your family and friends help to balance our lives. They provide a connection to your past, present and future by telling stories of shared experiences and their fondness for you. Similarly, you regale us with your meaningful stories about them and all those many escapades… cherished and remembered. To know your family and friends is to love you even more. **Today we share stories about our family and friends.**

JUNE 26

Music Creates the Mood

Music sets the tone for our moods and feeds our souls.

Most times when I walk into our home, you have music playing. It seems to be an extension of you, expressing how you feel at any given time. Sometimes the music is lively such as a world music song indicating your zest for life. Other times a new age melody or an adagio tempo is playing, suggesting a mood to slow down. I am revitalized when I recognize a lively electronic beat blaring from the stereo. Then again, silly comedic lyrics can fill me with a smile and lightness. **Today we create the musical ambiance we desire. Romance anyone?**

JUNE 27

Sharing

Offering each other our most prized item before first experiencing it shows caring.

When we reach to get the newspaper, we both want to be the first to read the sports page. However, you allow me to be the first to read it and patiently await your turn. You do that with so many things— such as letting me take the first shower or tasting a first bite of your favorite dish at a restaurant. Your thoughtful actions of sharing and giving encourage me to give to you and love you even more. So now it's your turn to read the sports section! **Today, I commit to sharing and letting you go first.**

JUNE 28

Praying Together

Starting the day with prayer.

Nearly all our lives, we have reserved saying prayers at bedtime. As adults, we would often say them silently when we came to bed at different times. Yet, when we jointly pray in the mornings, this is when I feel the closest to you. Our words are so sincere and filled with exquisite appreciation, compassion and love for God, our family, our brothers and sisters, and each other. We are so deeply touched by how caring we are and reminded each time of the blessings of gratitude in having each other in our lives. **Together we take time in the morning to experience an emotional and spiritual closeness of our sacred time together and to feel the blessings and abundance. We look for the miracles in our lives each day.**

JUNE 29

Taking Responsibility

When we take action, we are showing our love for our partner and ourselves.

Simple behaviors, such as making dinner reservations to ensure a romantic table, take little time on my part. Yet actions like this let you know that I care enough to prioritize a meaningful fun and enjoyable time together. Instead of expecting you to do things to please me, I take responsibility to create and maintain my own happiness. This increases my chances of being happier and radiates that happiness to you. Perhaps I volunteer to do a chore that you normally assume, or I may realize I am starting to feel run down, and ask for your assistance so I can rest for a while. **Today we each initiate an action or loving gesture that shows our love for ourselves and each other.**

JUNE 30

Loving Touch

We hold the power of love in our hands.

Today we take turns touching only the other's hand and arm while reclining. I slowly begin to stroke all the way up and down your arm to your hand. Then I work to change the tempo and firmness, alternating fast and slow, and soft and hard pressure. I might deftly use firm kneading, switch to gentle raindrops, and change again forming circles with the palms of my hands. I might even scratch you gently with my nails or do long strokes up and down your arms. Throughout this, you keep your eyes closed, delightfully absorbing changes in sensations… focusing only on the moment. You are free to enjoy without any performance on your part. We lovingly reciprocate. Oh, to savor for only a little longer!

july

JULY 1

Pictures

Photographs forever capture the moment.

Photographs serve as personal markers and milestones, and each runs parallel to our journey together. Too quickly one day passes into the next—without our stopping to appreciate what we were doing or how we looked. Years later, we stop and realize how many moments escaped without a photograph to remind us. A photo not only gives us a physical reminder of our appearance, but shows us how our children have grown and developed over the years. **Today we take pictures to preserve the beautiful images of our faces, bodies, and lives forever.** Photographs help us to preserve the events of the day, our relationships, and document unforgettable moments of our past, present and future together.

JULY 2

Giving Encouragement

When life is difficult, we are even more supportive of the other.

When life hands us lemons, we are there to lift each other's spirits with words and hugs. No matter how we may struggle with life's challenges, we are secure in knowing we can get through these trying times as long as we have each other. By asking the other to talk about emotional let downs, disappointments, and pressures, we offer life-sustaining encouragement. Listening without advice or judgment shows respect for each other and lets us know we have been heard. By not minimizing or ignoring concerns, emotions, or worries, we let others know it is okay to feel this way. Being overly reassuring is not our role. By being quiet and listening attentively, we provide encouragement, emotional support, and validation of feelings. We know that our lives will be stabilized and the problems rectified. **Today I ask you about any difficulties you may be facing and attentively listen without advice or solutions.** I love you and allow you enough time to talk to come up with your own solutions.

JULY 3

Choosing Colors

You color my days with sunshine.

What's your favorite color? As we get older, we may develop preferences for monochromatic colors, such as wanting to have our houses painted in white, brown, or gray. Our personalities have mellowed somewhat over time and we become indistinguishable, sometimes lost in the predictability of our daily lives. **This day, we discuss our favorite colors and how they are connected to our unique attributes**. Our individually chosen shades match our own characteristics and habits. In the fun of choosing from an array of colors to match our personalities, we become animated once more.

JULY 4

Independence Day

We give thanks for living in the greatest country in the world.

Each Independence Day, we seek a place to celebrate the vital freedom that generations before us fought so hard to attain. We stop to talk about how fortunate we are to be living at this point in history; especially how we are able to have the freedom to think, speak, write, and act upon our desires. Today we remember those who fought for these freedoms. We ask blessings for those who are still fighting for us and our country. **This day of independence gives us pause for appreciation to the contribution of others for us to live, work, and play together in our great nation**.

JULY 5

Enhancing Appearance

I take pride and joy in my appearance as a gift to both you and myself.

When you are freshly bathed and clothed in clean apparel that flatters your physique, I see the pride that you have in yourself and know that you are quite happy within yourself, causing my heart to flutter. I am as head over heels in love with you today as when we were dating. When you care enough about your appearance to maintain your attractiveness through appropriate eating, exercising, grooming, and tasteful dress, I find myself falling in love all over again. I love your face and body, no matter your age. You are the one who excites me and causes my heart to race. **Today, I take extra time with my grooming and appearance to please and attract you as if we were dating.**

JULY 6

Celebrating Our Interdependence

We must be complete within ourselves before we can truly become two people joined as one.

Our union was symbolized by a tree reaching to the sky, with its overlapping stems and branches intertwined. Years later, this metaphor is more fitting. We both have matured and become stronger, both individually and together. We now fully understand who we are as individuals, yet maintain our integrity rather than lose our sense of self simply to please the other. Undeniably, we are intertwined, working together, strengthening and bringing together synergistic energies that bring us closer still. Like the roots of trees that are interwoven beneath the earth's surface, our union and efforts are even more fortified. **Today we discuss and examine how independent we feel, and how we can help each other feel even more autonomous and interdependent.**

JULY 7

Resolving Anger, Sadness, And Hurt

I write my thoughts and feelings in a loving letter to you if I am angry, hurt, sad or disappointed.

Writing down my thoughts and feelings in letters to you helps when I feel dissatisfied with our relationship; clarifying how I may want to communicate with you. I'm able to understand these feelings more fully when I take time to look at what is causing them. When I am able to communicate with you in an open and direct way without accusations, blaming, or making assumptions about your motives, I am better at gaining your support and understanding. I add to your ability to understand my thoughts, feelings and what I want you to do to meet my needs and comfort me. **Today I examine my feelings to determine if there are any outstanding issues that I would like your assistance in resolving. I then write these feelings and the reasons behind them in a letter to you.**

JULY 8

Giving Recognition

You are outstanding in your field.

In our early days together, I would joke with you of how you were "outstanding in your field" due to your deep desire to be with nature and your dedicated efforts. You excel in your occupation and as a lover, friend, husband, and father. You are the best—and I am being totally objective!) **Today I acknowledge and recognize how you are outstanding in your career and in many other areas of life, both large and small.** You are full of innovative ideas— thinking out of the box to provide the best results whether it is about home, play, or work.

113

JULY 9

Writing Love Notes

The day you leave on a business trip I find a love note on my pillow.

Imagine how you would feel when your loved one goes on a business trip. You kiss and hug the night before and say loving words to each other. You may have your partner promise to wake you in the early morning hours—before slipping out the bedroom door. Is there time for one last kiss, hug, and another "I love you?" Yes, and more. **When I awakened this morning, there was a note of love on my pillow telling me how much I am already missed**. What a magical way to wake up and start the day!

JULY 10

Cuddling

We cherish the times when we are physically close.

There is a large sectional sofa in our home so we can easily spread out. However, we prefer to cuddle on only one end of this roomy sofa, scrunched up together, with our bodies overlapping each other. In this manner, we can be close as we watch television, listen to music, or just talk. Sometimes our whole family, including our daughter and beloved dog, are all huddled together at the end of the sectional sofa. What a funny sight it is! Yet these are some of the most endearing times we spend together as a family. **Today we cozy up to one another on a favorite piece of furniture.**

JULY 11

Sending Love

I send you my love and positive energies when I sense your sorrows and turmoil.

I take a moment to close my eyes and visualize whether there are any black, gloomy clouds around my heart. If there are any, I can then gradually replace them with a pure, bright white light that breaks through and dissipates the clouds. Darkness, doubt, sadness, and anxiety are slowly vaporized, and the white light comes shining through. After I experience emotional comfort and stability, I picture any dark clouds that may be surrounding your heart; these are displaced by my love. I send you the same pure bright light to encourage you and give you peace. May your heart be lightened of its burdens as you sense and feel the care and strength I send you. **Today we perform this exercise for ourselves and one another.**

JULY 12

Playing

Come play with me, today and every day.

As adults, we often become too serious about how we manage our daily lives: jobs, family, and home responsibilities. We forget to play, or take time to replenish our spirits and add freshness to our lives. **Today we take a short break to do something fun... perhaps to play a game, draw, dance and sing, do a little cheer, or flirt with each other**. Playing keeps us young. Our relationship is refreshed and renewed once more.

JULY 13

Friendships

Friends are our connection to relationships outside ourselves.

How long has it been since we've been together with our closest friends? We dream of being kids again, squealing with laughter... joking... teasing... jumping, hugging, and dancing. As a couple, we accept that neither of us can fulfill all of our individual needs, because we have different interests and personal characteristics. We need friendships with others. **Today I call a friend and set a date, eagerly anticipating getting together to have some fun, exchange stories, and catch up on our lives.** As we discuss our individual activities with friends, we might decide we also want to get reacquainted with another couple to have fun and deepen our relationship with them.

JULY 14

Being Spontaneous

To be flexible is to be alive and willing to change.

We can become so set in our ways. Ritualistic behaviors slowly creep into our lives, causing us to be somewhat robotic, almost as if on some sort of automatic pilot. **Today, we dare to change, to upset our nice little balance by introducing a new behavior to our daily routine to deepen our love.** Perhaps it is simply reading this affirmation together.

JULY 15

Getting Organized

I prioritize getting our home clean and orderly.

Our lives and home can become chaotic. I know how much you love organization. I can see how much you dislike the game of "hide and seek," which may consume hours or days of frantically looking for missing objects. I assist you in making organization a priority since I know it is important to you. Starting with a small area, we work together until we can see progress. Your encouragement motivates and sustains me to pick up items as I use them and put them away. **Today we start with small steps to clean and reorganize.** Rearranging our home is a project that benefits us both. Without your supportive plodding, I may habitually stash my "valuables." However, with you working alongside me, I am inspired to sort, release, throw out, and donate. Our home remains more beautifully organized and maintained.

JULY 16

Counting Our Blessings

I am filled with a deep sense of gratitude.

Sometimes we forget to stop and count our blessings as we rush to accomplish one important task after another. However, when we take a vacation, I thank God for not only getting us to our destination safely and for granting us an incredibly wonderful life, with the ability to enjoy the pleasures of travel. I am simply awe struck by the unbelievable beauty that encompasses us, soothing and invigorating our souls. We thank you, God, for blessing us with Your many graces. **Whether we travel or not, we take time today to count our blessings and feel embraced by a higher spirit.**

JULY 17

Being Intimate

Our bodies fit perfectly together when making love.

There is a bit of a difference in our heights. Yet this has never mattered in our sexual interludes. God created us to fit together perfectly. While we clsoely hold the other, our bodies, our love, and spirit join as one. Your breath quickens as does mine—our hearts race, and our bodies tighten and mirror the pacing of the adrenaline rush as we anticipate the ecstasy of climax. We are indeed undeniably perfect together! **Today we take time to fully appreciate the ways our bodies respond in tune with the other.**

JULY 18

Sharing and Trusting

You have been with me in my most private moments.

You hold and keep my deepest secrets, as you are my true and ultimate confidant and friend. I trust you with my most heartfelt thoughts, feelings, and actions. If I reveal information which disturbs you, instead of becoming agitated or short with me, you show acceptance and appreciation for my courage when I tell the truth by maintaining direct eye contact, nodding, smiling, hugging, holding my hand, and encouraging me to talk. Thank you for accepting me the way I am. **Today we share a "secret" we want to reveal.** I promise to hold your private secrets close to my heart.

JULY 19

Proclaiming Our Love

I love the way you say "I'm the luckiest man alive to have such a wonderful wife!"

When we've been at gatherings for business or with friends, you lovingly look at me and loudly proclaim to those standing close by, "Look at this woman! I'm the luckiest man alive!" When I hear those special words... I instantly feel both humbled and so completely loved and adored by you. I want you to also have this same exhilarating feeling. I want the whole world to know that I am married to the most incredibly wonderful man that has ever existed. I can't say enough about your virtues! **Today I joyfully exclaim, "I am the luckiest _____ alive to be with this _____! Imagine what a conversation starter this might be."**

JULY 20

Sharing Tasks

I show you my love each day by willingly sharing responsibilities at home.

When we first married, we made a list of all the tasks that had to be done at home. Then we divided the list equally, preferring to share all we did. By doing so, we were able to treat each other with consideration and love. Shared responsibilities not only provide us with the reward of more quickly completing the task but of having extra time together. As our family grows, it becomes even more important to share tasks so that we can enjoy more quality time together. **Today we enjoy engaging in our household responsibilities together and feel a greater sense of mutual respect and teamwork.**

JULY 21

Giving Cards

We carefully examine each note until our sentiments are revealed.

We joyfully pour over the vast selection of greeting cards, looking for exactly the right one that communicates just how deeply we love one another. Through the years, we have lovingly exchanged thousands of cards. In looking through them, it's revealing that the most popular cards that we give to each other are consistently romantic... even now. We treasure giving and receiving cards from each other knowing how much time and energy went into finding and writing special heartfelt messages in them. **Today we take time to find a card which expresses exactly what we want our loved one to know.**

JULY 22

Touching

My skin is the largest organ of my body and it hungers for your touch.

I feel a variety of emotions when you touch me. I sometimes feel shivers of excitement when you touch my skin. Other times your touch relaxes and calms me, hastening my sleep. You frequently make me laugh when you tickle me, and I curl up to protect myself from your playful torture. You also rely on deep kneading strokes to penetrate my muscles, at times causing my body to tighten. **Please touch me today and every day. In turn, I promise to touch your body, mind, and spirit.**

JULY 23

Cooking

The way to a man's heart is through his stomach.

I love to cook for you as this is a creative way to show how much I love you. You are my number one connoisseur, who eagerly tastes whatever I prepare for you and regularly lavish me with appreciative compliments. Your appreciation and kudos perpetually keep me wanting to please you even more. Food is love, and I love cooking for you! Bon appétit! Today I prepare a meal knowing my loving thoughts and actions are vital ingredients for the recipe of devotion.

JULY 24

Pampering

If you awaken before me, you bring home a cup of coffee and a sweet delicacy from the bakery.

How luxurious it is to sleep in on the weekends. You frequently indulge me, and I feel pampered when you quietly steal away, allowing me to rest for just a little longer. You then return with a nice steaming mug of coffee, prepared exactly the way I like it, and offer me a freshly baked treat. Come over so I can hug and kiss you… I'm yours! **Today I steal away while my partner sleeps.**

JULY 25

Singing

A favorite song comes on the radio, and you lip sync while romancing me with lyrics and gestures.

Singing is expressionistic and liberating. We can't be uptight and tense while singing. Instead we breathe in and out, taking big gulps of air as we belt out our favorite melodies. What truly makes singing so much fun is that we use songs to indicate how we're feeling or to remind us of our past. We cut up and gyrate until the other smiles and howls with laughter, drawing us ever closer. **Today we loudly sing a few songs together.** Do we serenade or sing off key?

JULY 26

Loving Life

I love my life!

Whenever I think of the words, "I love my life," which our child has repeated since she was young, I smile and completely agree. We do have a wonderful family, partners, and lifestyle. We are blessed to have so many gifts including closeness, communication, wonderment, love, health, exploration, and learning. **Today we express gratitude for our many blessings, while we enthusiastically announce to each other, "I love my life!"**

JULY 27

First Meeting

The first time I ever saw your face, my heart smiled.

I still remember the first time our eyes met. The world seemed to stand still and I was focused on every aspect of your being. I watched your eyes and your natural, engaging smile. I simply couldn't stop smiling or laughing at your jokes, your quick wit, and your engaging personality. I was quite smitten by you and could barely contain my excitement and joy. I felt happy, energetic, and hopeful. Time melted away so quickly. I didn't want that magical night to end and equally important—you didn't either. You were and are the most charming person I've ever met. **Today we reignite that sparkle of attraction when we first met, by intently watching each other's eyes and smiles as we share a favorite memory.**

JULY 28

Kissing

Kissing communicates "I want you," "I love you," and "I am passionate about you."

Today we experiment with our "kiss of the week." It's fun to try out short or long kisses, searching for the warmth of our mouths, finding our tongues dueling…and often passionately enmeshed together. Can I kiss you with my eyes open? Do I notice differences when they are closed? What do I notice when I hold you tight while kissing or have my hands behind my back? Can we communicate with each other using only our lips, mouths, and tongues? Let's find out and have some fun.

JULY 29

Mindful Loving

We choose the way we respond to each other.

By nature, we are predisposed to react... instead of automatically responding with criticism and blame, and anger with even more angry words and actions, we mindfully choose to look at various ways of responding to each other to produce the very best outcomes of love, harmony, acceptance, and closeness. When we are feeling angry and hurt, we may typically react with statements that wound by attacking each other. **Today we commit to doing our best to examine different meanings and perspectives when we become angry, hurt, threatened, or disappointed by each other**. By viewing actions and statements differently, we can better understand the other's true feelings and intentions.

JULY 30

Celebrating Anniversaries

We celebrate love, closeness, and growing together.

My life is totally and completely happy with you. I never realized I would meet someone who would utterly transform my life. We have become so united, close, and blissful in our marriage. I cherish each moment with you, feeling so blessed that we met each other. I believe the stars and the planets were completely aligned on that fortuitous day. **Today I recognize you, our special relationship, another year of our beautiful marriage, and give thanks for having you in my life.**

JULY 31

Writing Our Deepest Thoughts And Feelings

When we are stuck with overwhelming emotions, we write a loving letter to each other.

Sometimes my emotions and thoughts can be so intense that I find myself unable to fully express their magnitude in a meaningful way that can be readily accepted by you. I take the time today to start with a win-win statement of why I am writing this letter, such as "I am writing you, because I want us to be more loving and open with each other. I want to better express my feelings—just as I want to know yours." I then write my specific feelings and the thoughts behind them as I describe your behaviors which may contribute to my hurt, sadness, anger, disappointment, and fears. I conclude the letter by telling you what I appreciate about you, and I request specific actions that I would like from you, so you can assist me in working through the problems in our relationship. **Today we discuss our openness to writing each other a loving letter when we feel overwhelmed or stuck with our individual pain which prevents us from being intimate.**

august

AUGUST 1

Tears

Through moments of great sadness, you have been with me and comforted me.

Our lives have been magical and easily managed. Yet, there were times when we experienced some personal difficulties. During those experiences, you held me, listened to me, and comforted me with your touch, your wise words, and your physical presence. Thank you for always being there for me. **Today I show my gratitude to you for comforting me through a difficult time.**

AUGUST 2

Calling Parents

> **Today I call my parents to say, "Thank you and I love you."**

Children frequently take their parents for granted, assuming they will always be there for them. We look to our parents to lend assistance in meeting our needs and to fortify us with their love and assurances. Yet, without warning, we can lose the ones closest to us. **Today we honor our parents by calling them to express how much they are loved and appreciated**. Our parents have influenced us to become the adults we are. We recognize their importance in becoming the individuals we are and hope to become.

AUGUST 3

Exercise

> **You encourage me to exercise by giving up your free time to help me.**

You lovingly ask if I'm going to exercise today. You are not concerned about my appearance. Rather, your focus is primarily directed to my health, longevity, and total sense of psychological and physical well-being. I appreciate the way you care about me emotionally, mentally, and physically. By taking over some errands or child care responsibilities, you make it easier for me to exercise. **Thank you for sacrificing your free time for me.** This is a real commitment to me. Thank you, my love... I exercise to stay as healthy for both you and me.

AUGUST 4

Summer Vacations

The last days of summer are so sweet.

We savor the long days of summer, wishing somehow they would never end. **To extend the good times and the memories, we plan a family vacation.** We equally voice our opinions regarding where we'd like to go and what we'd like to do. A lively debate ensues with a vote on our destination. Now we have something to look forward to. The anticipation leaves us eager for the days to pass, buoying us for our intended journey.

AUGUST 5

Best Of The Best

You are by far my grandest gold medal winner.

You are in a category by yourself because you are the "best of the best." You are in a class all your own, confident to be your own person, secure to express and act upon what you believe is the best decision. You are honest, ethical, and fair, and you normally give others the benefit of the doubt. Most endearing to me is your unending love for our family. **Today I verbally award you the gold medal for** _____ **because** _____.

AUGUST 6

Femininity And Masculinity

We are psychologically healthier when we possess both male and female characteristics.

No longer do we have the notion of the stereotypical male or female qualities. Previously our concept of the traditional male was of one who was steadfastly quiet, very strong, and expressed little emotionally. Instead, we now see that we are happiest and emotionally healthy when we have a blend of male and female traits. We can be tender and strong, gentle and forceful, both a nurturer and a leader. We are free to break out of our molded definitions and simply be ourselves. **I give to you, my love, a blend of the best of both worlds.**

AUGUST 7

Celebrations

I celebrate each day with you.

Each day I spend with you calls for a celebration. It's too long to wait for a special occasion. We're overjoyed with our daily life together. Let's make a toast to our continued happiness or perhaps to an accomplishmenat that was finally realized today. We might spontaneously dine out for no particular reason… except that we're madly in love with each other. It may be a single rose you bring home to greet me and welcome the long weekend ahead. Every day is meaningful because of you. **Today we create a celebration of our love.** Perhaps it is using the dishes we reserve for company as we enjoy our meal at our fancy dining table or our casually romantic and serene patio. We might toast each other, or simply jump up and down as we hug.

AUGUST 8

Meditation

Exercise can be meditation time.

Monotony and boredom are part of swimming laps. However, swimming is my source of tranquility, a space to meditate, to rev up my creative juices, to feel gratitude, and to pray. As I automatically stroke and kick my legs, my thoughts may turn to unfinished business that occupies my mind. Effortlessly, solutions come into my brain, sometimes so brilliantly that I attribute them from God. I believe my life is a miracle and I am filled with gratitude-- I thank God for the abundance of wealth in love, health, lifestyle, my ability to help people, and meaningful prayers. Swimming renews my closeness with God and my gratitude for His multitude of favors. **Today I swim (or engage in another sustained exercise) with full intentions of giving gratitude to all that exists in my life.**

AUGUST 9

Simple Pleasures

I relish the simple pleasures of daily life with you.

Today we bask in the privilege of living extraordinary lives— smiling at each other as we get ready in the mornings, offering a quick hug before breakfast or hopping in the car, and being delighted by the little conversations we share throughout the day. Of course, the hugs and kisses before we end our day are always welcomed. Tonight before bedtime, we take a few minutes to sit in our backyard lounge chairs looking at the stars and the majesty of the night. We stare at the moon, the shape of the constellations, and the silhouettes of our incredible environment. Life is so remarkable! Together we have everything we want and need.

AUGUST 10

Playfulness As Quality Time

Playing cards and board games settles us in for the night.

Some leisurely activities may cost too much. Financially, we may not be able to partake in a past-time we crave. **To find a solution, today we discuss and decide on games we used to enjoy in times past.** Perhaps it is a game of charades, a board game—with lady luck on our side—or playing cards. Whatever the activity, it is meaningful for you and our family to share some fun and quality time tonight.

AUGUST 11

Affirmations

We create affirmations to strengthen our relationship and set goals.

Today as we talk with each other, we determine goals we would like to achieve as a couple. We each write down at least three affirmations, which are positive statements about how we want to achieve our desired outcomes. For instance, instead of saying that I don't want to argue with you, I might use an affirmation that states, I am enjoying a closer relationship with my mate by openly communicating my innermost thoughts and feelings as they arise. By personalizing and recording affirmations, we generate a powerful belief and amazing force of energy. These affirmations assist our minds in accomplishing anything we can imagine.

AUGUST 12

Prayer

A nightly family prayer together brings us closer to God and to each other.

Together we commit to saying prayers whether at mealtimes or at night, to anchor us spiritually as a family. By each of us saying our prayers out loud, we reinforce the deep love, admiration, and gratitude we hold for God, one another, and for the beautiful blessings in our lives. These are revered times in prayer where we draw closer to God and one another by hearing each other's appreciation for our family, health, love, guidance, people in our lives, careers, and school.

AUGUST 13

Openness To Love

I appreciate and fall in love with creatures I first abhorred.

From the beginning, you have been fascinated with creatures great and small. Some of these animals were cold blooded, and generally believed to be unfit as household pets. Yet you persuaded me to take them—one by one—into our home. Somehow a transformation occurred within me where I actually began to care for these strange creatures and enjoyed the novelty of them as household pets. I would even hold them, stroking them while I soothingly spoke to them. The miracle of love transforms us all. **Today we open our minds to all of God's creatures who can teach us lessons of life and love.**

AUGUST 14

Boundaries

In love, we respect the other's boundaries.

Boundaries are physical and emotional forms of protection and guidelines for behaviors. A physical boundary may involve being distant when I'm angry with you, or when I need to be alone. It could also include allowing in our personal space, only those persons we trust and with whom we feel a sense of safety. **Emotionally, when I say no, you show that you respect my boundary by accepting my thoughts, feelings, and needs without manipulating me to change my mind.** By respecting each other's boundaries, our love knows no limits.

AUGUST 15

Affection

We openly and spontaneously demonstrate affection to each other in the presence of our child.

Feeling a bit uncomfortable is quite possible when we show affection in front of our children. A consequence may be that our children may not learn how to demonstrate deep love when engaged in adult relationships. We, as parents, are the models and the ultimate guides for our children. We are the first symbols of love for each other and for them. **Today we resolve to freely share our love with one other in a natural and open manner, modeling a loving relationship for our children.**

AUGUST 16

Brushing Your Hair

I am reclining, my head in your lap as you soothingly brush my hair.

As infants, we were coddled and our hair was brushed tenderly by our caregivers with a soft bristled brush. That stroking relaxed us, hypnotizing us into a lull... our bodies becoming limp. With you, my love, I can truly let down my guard and become tranquilized by your caring touch as you languidly brush my hair, massaging my head with every stroke. I am in heaven. Thank you, my love. **On this day, we gently and lovingly brush or massage the other's scalp.**

AUGUST 17

Depersonalizing

I embrace your behaviors even when they annoy me.

In every relationship, there comes a time, no matter how much we love our mates, that some habits become irritating to us. During those times we must look within ourselves to see what it is about the other that is affecting us so negatively. Sometimes we find that we take these behaviors personally, as though our loved one is directly doing this to annoy us. From this day forth, I remind myself this is the person I love, and this is who he is; it is not about me. **I accept and embrace all the qualities that make you my sweetheart.**

AUGUST 18

Our World Astounds Us

We are open to the magic around us.

We see the magnificent world around us in the mountains, trees, meadows, lakes, desert, and open plains. Just like our relationship, we take time to explore what's underneath the surface. When we are underwater, we are introduced to another world of fauna and flora, with creatures that disguise themselves in mysterious and ingenious ways. Sunlight streams into crystal clear turquoise waters with fish small and large, squid, turtles, and eels. Corals invite us to study their colors and textures while they masquerade as rocks and plants. We are weightless and free, swimming with the creatures of the sea, and all is wonderful with our world. **Today we explore an uncharted territory for ourselves.** Perhaps we explore a stream, lake, ocean, or pool with snorkel and goggles, or we might take a hike to an area that is new to us – to discover animals that quickly hide as we approach different plant forms residing underneath larger protective plants. We excitedly discuss our discoveries.

AUGUST 19

Parenting

You are a remarkable parent.

Many times I watch with amazement and admiration as you spend time with our child. Early on—it was the way you held her, caressed her, and stroked her hair, cheeks, and arms or kissed her so tenderly and gently. Later on—it was the way you talked, joked, and encouraged her. Conversations were lively and educational at dinner or while you helped her with homework. You would be playful and spend hours immersed in games, crafts, or exploring the world outdoors. Later, you would return with stories and gleeful treasures you found abounding in our neighborhood. You are a wonderful parent! How blessed our child is to have you. **Today I look for ways you are an exceptional parent as you engage in everyday activities with our child**. I acknowledge and compliment specific behaviors that I have noticed and thank you, feeling even more proud of you and feeling even closer to you.

AUGUST 20

Precious

You are so precious to me.

Above all things, we want to feel cherished. The desire to feel precious is a natural, human need. If you ever believe that you are not precious and prioritized by me, please tell me gently, firmly, and directly describing how you perceive my actions. I promise to listen. **Today I communicate precisely what is so special about you and the effect you have on me as I explain your virtues.**

AUGUST 21

Healing Touch

I touch you with healing energy.

I cannot cure your physical maladies. Yet I can help you to feel more comfortable. When your neck is stiff or sore, I can knead the surrounding tissues and press and rub trigger points that stimulate your body's own healing process. By simply touching, I am sending positive messages to your nerve endings to enjoy, relax, and release. **Today I ask you if there is a part of your body that needs attention, and I lovingly touch and soothe that area to promote healing and comfort.**

AUGUST 22

Beautifying Our Home

Together we beautify our home.

Sometimes, when we shop together for plants, we look for just the right ones to provide the perfect color, or foliage, or texture. Other times, jointly we search for furniture, carpet, appliances, tiles, or other household items to transform our house into our dream home. No matter what we do together to improve our home, it's great to plan and work as a team. It's the sharing of dreams come true. **Today we discuss plans to create even more beauty for our home.**

AUGUST 23

Sex

We physically express our love.

Sex is more than a physical act. As an act of love it encompasses the key ability to communicate nonverbally how you are the person with whom I want to share my body, mind, and spirit. It is God's greatest expression of a man and a woman being physically and emotionally intertwined and giving of one's self. **Today we share this ultimate closeness.** When we gave our bodies to each other, we were united forever as God lovingly blessed us.

AUGUST 24

Being Nostalgic

We go to a drive-in movie and are transported back in time.

Remember the fun we had as kids, piling into the car in our pajamas, the back seat laden with blankets and pillows? We'd pull into the parking space, hook the speaker onto the car window, and head for extra treats from the snack bar. It seemed we could not get enough snacks—even smuggling in extra food and drinks to keep us happy and occupied throughout the double feature. We sat enthralled by the movies, blissfully falling asleep, without a care in the world, secure that life couldn't get any better than this. **Tonight we share a nostalgic moment by piling our blankets and treats in front of our TV and allowing ourselves to enjoy drifting off, happily full and satisfiled with our world..**

AUGUST 25

Falling In Love

Each time I look at you I fall in love all over again.

My eyes cannot drink in enough visions of you. You are larger than life to me and while looking at you... I am flooded with a thousand beautiful memories of our fun times, romantic interludes, and emotional closeness. Even after all these years, I can't believe you're mine. When I think of you, I feel I am the most fortunate person in the world to have you in my life. Every day, and every gesture and word from you are stored in my mind. **Today I talk about your characteristics and behaviors that promote my falling in love with you more each day.**

AUGUST 26

Hope

You give me hope when I doubt myself.

There are times when even my bountiful optimism diminishes, wondering when events will flow in a more encouraging direction. You are there with me... intently listening to my concerns and understanding my discouragement. Being by my side, you show me through your words and action that you respect my feelings. As long as we are together, we will get though any hardships facing us. During this difficulty, you help me realize how powerful your love is for me and that these times are only temporary. You provide me with hope for better days ahead. **Today we share our struggles, providing support for each other by listening and showing that we hear and understand.** Physical support is also demonstrated by stroking the back, hugging, or holding each other—conveying messages, "I love you" and "I am with you."

AUGUST 27

Reliving Our Marital Commitment

Our wedding cemented our never ending love.

When we wed, and said "I do," God smiled on us and the angels sang. Our hearts soared estatically at our union. We were both tearful, and our throats tightened as we simultaneously experienced incredible elation. **Today we re-live that deep commitment to God and each other, forever encircled with a love that grows deeper every day.** We exchange our thoughts and feelings about what our marriage means to us as we take the time to hold hands and look into each other's eyes as we did on our wedding day.

AUGUST 28

Being Equal

You and I are equal partners.

Power is a word that is often used in relationships. We are united in all our sharing and decision-making. We allow the other freedom to make decisions. Neither of us is dominant nor passive. Paradoxically, we seem to get "our way" the majority of the time. Happiness is best when shared. When I help you attain your desires—then you are indefatigable in helping me achieve mine. **We are life partners who create win-wins situations and are open to compromising to help both of us be happier.**

AUGUST 29

Laughing

We revive the long carefree days of youth by laughing until it hurts.

Summer vacations were all about packing in as much as we could. That meant trying to chuckle and laugh as much as we could each day. We'd sleep in late because we were tired from watching so much television late in the evenings or talking for hours at sleepovers. Sometimes we'd surprise ourselves and wake up at the crack of dawn. There were no school bells threatening to mute our enthusiasm. We'd play hard and get punchy, getting a case of the sillies, turning everything we said or did into wild spasms of laughter. We would watch slapstick comedies from the past just to see who would laugh the hardest. What fun! **Today we recapture the magic of youth by looking for humor in everyday activities.**

AUGUST 30

Surprise Getaway

I take pleasure in surprising you with a romantic, fun-filled getaway.

I enjoy such pleasure in packing your clothes and belongings for a secret vacation. Our getaway might be for a weekend, or even longer. Each time you reward my efforts with a smile, hugs, and kisses. You quickly and easily express your surprise and affection with words of gratitude. It is a delight to plan such a journey for you. I look forward to spending time alone with you—one of my greatest joys in life. **Today I plan a surprise get away for us, eagerly anticipating your reactions as you discover what I'm up to!**

AUGUST 31

Forgiving

We are imperfect—yet perfect for each other.

We make mistakes. When we do, we must have the courage to admit to each other that we were wrong, apologizing about specific behaviors and statements that may have wounded the other. **Today, I look at ways I may have harmed you by not hearing and recognizing your needs, and I ask for your forgiveness. In return,** I ask you to do the same. I want us to be close by letting go of past anger and hurt.

september

SEPTEMBER 1

Communication

> **I communicate my thoughts and feelings to you as I become aware of them.**

In my family of origin, I learned to keep my thoughts and feelings inside and solve my own problems. I also realized early in our marriage that suppressing my feelings was unhealthy—not only for me, but also for our relationship. I might be inclined to over-react about seemingly insignificant events. Now we've changed our behaviors to communicate directly when either of us becomes cognizant of any thoughts and feelings damaging to our intimacy. By talking freely, we are able to handle our emotions when we are calm. This leads to better communication skills. The possibilities are endless as we grow individually and together, when we keep the lines of communication open. **I commit to talking to you in a calm manner as I become aware of my thoughts, feelings, and needs.**

SEPTEMBER 2

Awareness

You provide the missing piece of information about me.

Sometimes we're not able to see ourselves the way others see us. This is where you are very perceptive and insightful. You are able to describe how I may come across when I say something. You suggest alternative actions that I might take. You also help me to see how others may be affected by what I say and do. Thank you for allowing me to see my blind side the way only you can see it. You communicate in a loving, helpful way to encourage me to understand and change my behavior. **Today we fill in the details about information of which we may be unaware.**

SEPTEMBER 3

Growing And Changing

Our love goes through seasons of change.

In the beginning, we peeked at each other, wonder-eyed and uncertain of what might lay ahead for us. Our relationship began to bud as we exchanged glances, words, and later touch and affection. As we revealed ourselves and risked being vulnerable with our emotions, our love blossomed like flower petals unfolding toward the light. In the summer season, wildlife and plants are at their peak, nurturing their families and putting forth energies to create fruits. Similarly, we seem to hit our stride, finding a sense of security and comfort in the other's love and actions. If we begin to take the other for granted—or stop acknowledging and appreciating each other, we stop growing as a couple. Individually and together we start withering, lacking the energy or resources to stop the erosion of our union. **Today, we protect our relationship and our love by defining what we love about each other.**

SEPTEMBER 4

Birthdays

Your birth is a day of celebration, a miraculous day when you appeared from the heavens.

On this day, I celebrate your birth and the remarkable person you have become. You are thoughtful, loving, dedicated, well-mannered, and mature. I often enjoy how you openly—and constructively—express many of your emotions… while emanating fun with a hint of mischief. Also, you are talented, intelligent, creative, and hard working. You consistently strive to do your best. You are a humble man who keeps his word, is honest, and a person who relates to all whom you meet. You are also a leader and a visionary at times. All in all, I would say you are a perfect fit for me! Happy Birthday, my darling! My sweetheart, what a better time than birthdays, for me to regale you with your special qualities – and thank you for the gift of your life!

SEPTEMBER 5

Dates

We prioritize our times for sexual intimacy by setting dates.

We have dates for romantic pursuits such as dining out, going to the movies, a concert, or even a ball game. Why not set a date for sex—the most intimate, physical activity between us? Days pass and sex may become neglected due to our individual exhaustive schedules or the incompatibilities of when we each retire for the evening. **To honor our union, we pick a time and place for our sexual interlude.**

SEPTEMBER 6

Security

Interacting with an attractive person of the opposite sex, we feel secure in our love.

At times, we may feel threatened or even jealous whenever either of us engage in conversations with another member of the opposite sex. Instead, I am comfortable with how you show me you love, devotion, and loyalty every day. I feel fully secure when you are with me or away from me. I trust you completely not to take any action that would harm our relationship. I am the recipient of your undying love, the one you come home to at night, and the one who has your undivided attention. I want you to be yourself around all people, just as you want me to be free to be myself. **Today I remain secure with your love, devotion, and faithfulness when you are with other persons.**

SEPTEMBER 7

Climbing Mountains

When we hike mountain trails together, it symbolizes we can accomplish any goal.

Steadily making progress, we are more deeply united and frequently feel a great sense of pride in our accomplishments, even when cimbing uphill is exhausting and tedious. The journey tests our character and defines the ways we treat one another. This is especially true when we are faced with challenges. We reach the mountain peak, feeling exhilaration and relief. We can accomplish anything when we have the other at our side. **Today we face a physical challenge together as a metaphor of our partnership in achieving goals.**

SEPTEMBER 8

Entertaining

Teamwork makes entertaining family and friends enjoyable.

Whenever we entertain family and friends in our home, we work as a team. You are right there by my side cleaning the house and preparing for our guests. I notice how diligently you work to ensure the pool, patio, and yard present a showplace to be proud of. In the kitchen, you assist with cooking and arranging food trays and beverages. You are absolutely my partner in everything we do. Even tasks around the house bring us closer together. **Now we sit back and enjoy the festivities together.**

SEPTEMBER 9

Illness

You comfort me when I'm ill.

Sadly, no one can cure the ills of the other. Yet, the very nature of your thoughtfulness helps cheer me and adds to my comfort. You ask how I feel, and by bringing me water, hot teas, juices, or cold compresses to soothe my aches, I am free to rest. I feel your care and concern and I am comforted, knowing you help me to a speedier recovery. **Today I remind myself to be tender and attentive the next time that you are ill by asking how you feel and offering assistance.**

SEPTEMBER 10

Changing Routines

Today we add a unique element to our lives.

We frequently go day after day, caught in the same routine. Today... we make a small, deliberate change which may be designed to enhance our relationship. It could be something as simple as meeting at the coffee shop, taking a walk together in the morning before work, falling asleep to music, or going to bed a half hour earlier to snuggle and talk. **Today we take action to create a new behavior in our lives to keep our relationship fresh and add new diversions to our lives.**

SEPTEMBER 11

Acting Silly

We become old when we act our age.

Nothing is better than being silly and playful with you. We love to giggle and laugh like a couple of kids sharing some personal joke or playing tricks on the other. You have made me smile and laugh more than anyone in my entire life, and I love you for that. Perhaps it's that crazy way you make faces, unable to hide your true feelings. **Today I do something zany and unpredictable to create merriment in our lives.**

SEPTEMBER 12

Love

Loving you comes naturally.

Many people work too hard to show their affection and love to another. With you, my love flows naturally and freely. Being in love with you is playful, connected, and a masterful blend of emotions, intellect, spirit, and physical expression. I bend toward you as a plant to the sun. You return my efforts tenfold. **Today I spontaneously show my love by watching your cues.** Do I notice you're tired or not feeling quite right? Do you need assistance with taking out the garbage—or some project? Are you eager to talk about your day or worries, or are you needing to have a quiet time alone? I look, listen, sense, and learn the many signals you send me.

SEPTEMBER 13

Finances

Talking about our monthly budget helps us pay bills and plan our financial goals.

Financial pressures can destroy the loving bonds between us. The pressures can become constant—ubiquitous, and slowly yet steadily creep into our daily lives. Having equal input and involvement about our personal budget, we communicate regularly, regardless of which of us is bringing home the paycheck. We both seek financial harmony by establishing common goals and rules such as agreeing on purchases or sticking to a budget for dining and entertainment. We willingly give recognition and thanks for each other's contributions. **Today we discuss our bills for next month so we can plan our expenses and income, enhancing our ability to cooperate and fully engage each other.**

SEPTEMBER 14

My Hero

You are my hero.

When I think of heroes, you are my greatest. You are the person that I most look up to, the person whom I admire, and who has taught me so much about life, love, and myself. You so freely give me love, and you are the person that I want to confide in. You are my model for being open with others as you easily initiate conversations and listen attentively to their responses. Your actions also show sincerity, integrity and patience. **Today I tell you the many reasons you are my hero.**

SEPTEMBER 15

Stretching

We help each other stretch from head to toe.

Whatever we do, it seems as if we accomplish more if we work together. **Today we help each other stretch, imitating the skills of a professional trainer for elite athletes, to relieve tensions and to increase flexibility.** I gently pull and stretch you to reach your maximum range of motion as you embrace the physical contact. We are invested in each other's health so we may stay strong and stress-free.

SEPTEMBER 16

Cooperation

When I want to change a habit, I ask for your assistance.

Certain pesky behaviors have a way of detracting us from being connected and getting in the way of our personal happiness. That is why I want you to know that I am grateful for the support you give me when learning new, more productive behaviors. These habits can be as mundane as chewing nails or tapping fingers. Other ingrained actions might need to be addressed. These can be more significant such as reducing alcoholic drinking, spending less money, or changing eating habits to promote a healthier lifestyle. **Today I ask for your help in making changes big and small, because you are so much a part of my life.**

SEPTEMBER 17

Healthy Me

I honor myself so that I may honor you.

Loving and accepting the way I am, and willingly acknowledging both my strengths and weaknesses, is the truest manner of honoring myself. When I appreciate the way I really am, I am freer to accept you for who you are. There is no need to try to change you. **Today I let go of my efforts to make you become the person I think you should be or change to the way I want you to be.** I recognize that neither of us is perfect, yet we both have strengths which outweigh any weaknesses. I love both you and me for the unique individuals we are.

SEPTEMBER 18

Books

Reading allows us to dream, and escape to another world.

We have both spent so many wonderful hours at the library and bookstore looking for books together, reading to each other, and to our child. We share a genuine thirst for increased knowledge, mystery, excitement, fantasy, adventure, and romance. Perhaps we look for travel books for our next vacation destination. Other books may provide fresh ideas for greater romance or fun. **Today we visit our local library or bookstore to find a book to read together**.

SEPTEMBER 19

Words Of Love

I long to hear your words of love.

We whisper familiar terms of endearment and words of love when we snuggle, caress, or kiss. We never tire of the words "I love you," "you're just right for me," or "you're the most important person in my life." Thank you, my love, for brightening my day… for brightening my life. **Today we exchange words of endearment and love—creating even more love.**

SEPTEMBER 20

Eternity

You are the one that I chose to spend the rest of my life with.

When we were younger, we sometimes discussed growing old together. We've now been together for many years, and you are the one that still makes my heart jump. You are the first one that I want to see in the morning and the last one at night... and all of our moments in between. Our years together keep getting better as we consciously choose to love one another and show signs of thoughtfulness each day. **Today I tell you, "You are the one that I want to spend the rest of my life with."**

SEPTEMBER 21

Thoughtfulness

I bring you a cold beverage when I see you hot, sweaty, and working hard.

Often our love is measured in how we make the best use of kind gestures to demonstrate our deep love to each other. When the sun is beating down on you, your shirt becomes soaked, and your face is turning red, I bring you a frosty beverage to show you my love and appreciation. You didn't have to work in the yard or patio today, but you are trimming and scrubbing to make our home even more glorious. **Today I thank you for caring and working so hard on your day off.** You are indeed showering me with your kindness and with your devotions of love.

SEPTEMBER 22

Picnic

Few things in life are better on a sunny afternoon than to be lying with you on the grass... talking, eating, drinking, and lazily watching the clouds go by.

The more the pace of our hectic lives speeds up, the more we consciously slow ourselves down. We do that by having a picnic in our favorite park, our backyard, or a scenic lakeside retreat. With deliberation, we spread out on blankets, our bodies nestled together, as we munch on tasty treats and sip delicious cool drinks. Delighting in the day, we watch the formation of billowy clouds, labeling their shapes as they drift by. From time to time, we lose the consciousness of the other's words and thoughts as our heavy eyes close in perfect peace. **Today we enjoy a leisurely picnic to replenish ourselves and lazily enjoy the other's company.**

SEPTEMBER 23

Annoying Habits

We are imperfectly perfect.

Both of us exhibit behaviors from time to time—actions which neither likes or is wholeheartedly endorsed.. Over the course of time these annoying behaviors can become magnified. When these irritating behaviors arise, we remind ourselves that we are imperfect. We all make mistakes. We can become reactive, allowing our primitive primal side to take over our minds and actions. **Today we consciously let go of judgments and allow both of us to make mistakes, knowing that we glean valuable information from them**. Only then can we be truly accepting and loving of ourselves and each other.

SEPTEMBER 24

Telephone Greetings

We use words of endearment when greeting each other.

When the other calls, we are greeted with "Hi, my love" or "Hi sweetheart." These loving words are music to our ears since no one else uses these particular phrases of endearment in quite the same tone. Just starting our conversations this way, seems to set the mood for a warmer, cooperative, more stimulating discussion. We almost always close with "I love you" -- a perfect ending indeed. **Today we start by calling our loved one with special words of endearment.**

SEPTEMBER 25

Kissing

Today we kiss passionately as if we haven't kissed in a month!

Oh, the wonderful kiss! I love the way we hold each other and kiss. The warmth of our lips, our mouths, and our breaths helps us savor this amazing moment of intimacy. We close our eyes and let the sensations mingle and build into passion. Kiss me again and don't stop! **Today we kiss as if we were starved for each other's kisses. Does this merit "the kiss of the month?.**

SEPTEMBER 26

Pride

When I watch you perform, my heart swells with pride.

Whether you are presenting at a meeting or performing at a recital, my throat becomes tight, my eyes water, and my heart pounds for you. I am so proud of you. No matter what you do, you are my brightest star. You touch me with your grace, composure, talent, and ability to achieve miraculous feats. **Today I acknowledge how proud I am of you no matter what you do.**

SEPTEMBER 27

Feeding

I lovingly feed you.

Our parents lovingly and patiently fed us tiny spoons full of food when we were babies. We display the same type of tenderness by taking turns feeding each other. Sometimes we use our fingers to pick up a morsel and gingerly place it into our lover's mouth. Other times we slowly place spoons full of delectable tastes into our hungry mouths while we teasingly exaggerate the deliberate withdrawal. **This day we experiment with different textures and tastes—salty, sweet, sour, or bitter—combining them into flavorful delights.** We kiss and lick any stray crumbs from our lips.

SEPTEMBER 28

Cherished

I treat you tenderly because you are the most precious person in the entire world.

The more I love you, the more you flourish as a person. As I compliment you... you smile and acknowledge my words. You brighten up, looking for ways to repay the compliment through your own words of praise and affection for me. Similarly you take action to demonstrate your loyalty, devotion, and love. Our love has come full circle. By cherishing you through my words and deeds, I am rewarded many times over. **Today we freely compliment and hold each other knowing whatever we give, our love is returned to us.**

SEPTEMBER 29

Moment To Moment

We live in the now.

Individually and together we live in the moment. We can waste too much time—worrying about our future, preventing us from living fulfilled lives. The present is here and gone in a second. We pause to savor the laughter and revealing conversations, and relax as waves of energy ebb and flow. Nothing is better than being with you right now. **Today we take the time to enjoy the "now" and dialogue about what we notice or appreciate about the present.**

SEPTEMBER 30

Being Silly

> **We rejoice in playfulness by taking silly photographs of each other.**

Sometimes when I try to snap a handsome picture of you, you quickly sneak in a clownish, lopsided broad grin, or contort your face in less than becoming ways. My emotions are mixed— I might experience minor annoyance, or I may be filled with sheer delight by your playful antics. When I pose attractively for a photo, you sabotage the shot by making me laugh hysterically. Now my photo shows me doubled over with laughter, my eyes barely open and my mouth askew. **Today we intentionally pose with our funniest expressions as we tickle, joke, and pan for the camera.**

october

OCTOBER 1

Viewing Sunsets

The majestic colors of a beautiful sunset reflected from the sky to the earth fill us with wonder.

Some of our most wonderous pleasures are sitting together at sunset mesmerized by the sun setting on the ocean. It appears to fall from the sky. We watch the sun change the hues of the mountains into yellows, blues, and magenta. Seemingly on top of the world, we hold hands, kiss, and hug as we take in nature and are filled with its blessings. **Today we celebrate the magnificence of God's beauty as we revel in our closeness.**

OCTOBER 2

Sharing A Perfect Day

We create our future.

We all hold dreams of what a perfect day would be like one, two, or five years from now. **Today we take the time to contemplate our perfect day.** We write down how our day would begin. What it looks, feels, smells, tastes, and sounds like in the future. Would we wake up nestled together and smelling the aroma of coffee? Or are we awakened with a gentle, yet rousing kiss—from the other or our child? Perhaps you hand me a glass of juice along with a single white rose in a crystal vase? What activity would we choose on our perfect day? Would we close our eyes and fall into a serene slumber after a peaceful time together? I look forward to sharing our dreams of the perfect day.

OCTOBER 3

Conscious Loving

Loving you is a conscious choice.

We both readily admit that our relationship, and how it evolved so magnificently, didn't happen accidentally. We cultivate love, on a daily basis, like a garden… knowing that relationships are the result of sustained effort.. Daily we share expressions of love by proclaiming our appreciation for each other. We complement each other lovingly. We may show our love by a physical and sexual embrace, actions that enrich and make life easier for our mates, voicing our appreciation of the other's efforts, and through the gifts of time and attention. Also, we might carefully select or create presents as surprises. Most importantly, we share ourselves and demonstrate that we fully support and understand. **We thoughtfully contemplate today and every day how we want to make our love flourish even more.**

OCTOBER 4

Exercise

Whenever I exercise, you encourage my efforts with loving comments.

Exercising on a regular basis is one of the hardest behaviors for us to initiate and maintain. However, each time I exercise, you still generously sprinkle compliments about the way my body is becoming toned, the great job I'm doing, and how I am becoming healthier. You also add humor to my workouts by writing funny notes about my level of progress or my frequency of exercise. Thank you for caring about my health and longevity. **Today we encourage each other to become more fit by doing exercises together.**

OCTOBER 5

Reliving Love Through Cards

Love cards from the past help us to recapture our romance, reminding us of our extraordinary love.

I eagerly anticipated receiving the precious messages of love from you when we were apart. I couldn't wait to open the card every time I spied either your address or distinctive handwriting. Tearing the envelope, I would voraciously soak in the words with both my mind and my heart. **Today, we together re-experience those unforgettable moments by sharing our cards saved over the years.** By knowing the reason for the selection and remembering how each written word was carefully chosen and totally heartfelt, we deepen our connection. Thank you, my love, for being the light in my life.

OCTOBER 6

Creating My Own Happiness

I am in touch with my needs and wants so I can create my own happiness.

I take charge of my emotions and am aware of what I desire. When I am in touch with my needs and wants, I am less likely to stray from doing what I believe I "should" do to create your happiness or add to your comfort. If I follow these "should's," then I am merely doing what I think is the socially correct and responsible behavior. I may rob myself of my own happiness, sacrificing myself and feeling in the end like a victim. If I helplessly jeopardize myself by not meeting my own needs and wants, I become unhappy and critical with you. **Today I ensure happiness in our relationship by attending to my own needs and wants whether that might be taking time to exercise, reading while others clean up after dinner, or going to bed early**.

OCTOBER 7

Passion

We rediscover "our song" and play it to each other.

We share a very special song that epitomizes our relationship. It signifies our unity, the powerful moments when we first met, held each other, kissed, and were first intimate. When we play our song, we become transported to our shared past, reawakening memories, emotions, and passion. **Today I want to be as passionate with you as when we were first courting.** I want to feel how it was when we found each other. We nurture our relationship step-by-step into the blissful miracle it is today.

164

OCTOBER 8

Being Apart

Whenever you go on a trip, my heart travels with you.

We can be physically apart, yet so near. Sometimes I picture where you might be—in your office, a restaurant, or a hotel in some far away city. I may say a quick prayer for you or send you my positive energies of hope and love. I sometimes think of the last things you said to me or the feel of our last embrace. Again, I feel a smile creeping across my face, and you are there with me. **Today I think of your heartfelt words and tender embraces when you are away from me.**

OCTOBER 9

Laughing

I laugh out loud thinking about your funny antics.

Sometimes when I am home alone, in the car, or at work, I begin to think about something you said or did last night. My face lights up with glee, and at times, I laugh until the tears flow, such as when you do a parody of what I say, accompanied by my gestures. Even when we are apart, I enjoy your spirit. **Today we think of humorous comments that the other has made and share them with each other.**

OCTOBER 10

Being Assertive

When I speak about my anger, I am assertive, not aggressive.

In the past, when I would let my anger overtake me, I would quickly blame, accuse, criticize, and try to convince you that my feelings were justified. I found myself using aggressive methods that would alienate you by "stepping on your toes." Now I simply state my feelings and thoughts in an honest way and ask that you listen. **Today I assert myself to let you into my deepest needs and desires.**

OCTOBER 11

Forgiving

I examine if I may have harmed you in any way and make amends.

Today we take the time to look inward to cleanse ourselves of resentment, bitterness, jealousy, or emotions, which resulted in our taking harmful actions against each other. This is a day for us to begin the healing process by being accountable for our behaviors. Neither of us are perfect... we vow to be kinder, more thoughtful, and honest. Above all we apologize and rectify all transgressions. Instead of blaming one another, we determine how we may have contributed to our loved one's hurt, sadness, or anger. By doing so, we free our soul and spirit to allow our love to truly manifest. We now start afresh to greet each other with forgiveness and love.

OCTOBER 12

Healing

Today we plan a symbolic forgiveness.

Sometimes, it is difficult for us to let go of a grievance. Perhaps, we may not have talked enough about a particular problem, or not received understanding and concern from each other. **Today we examine ways to symbolically help us remember we have closed the door on past issues.** That ritual may be planting a tree to symbolize that we are growing together, or to light candles and let them sail away on small floats on a lake or pond. It could even mean each of us trimming off strands of our hair to "bury the hatchet." These actions bring us a step closer to healing our past.

OCTOBER 13

Engaging In Physical Activities Together

We discuss common activities that we did long ago and commit to doing them now.

Recently we went on a hike to an awe-inspiring, natural travertine cave with a waterfall and realized we may not have the stamina or the physical skills to navigate climbing over slippery rocks and slopes as we age. We became alarmed that many of the pleasures that we take for granted and postpone for the future may not be available to us as we physically age. **Today we set a date to engage in an activity that we have long disregarded, to fully enjoy and appreciate our bodies while living in the present.**

OCTOBER 14

Creating Excitement

We playfully shop together and pick seductive apparel.

We shop together and assist each other to select flattering and rather seductive apparel. As we playfully model sensual garments, we engage in a rating scale reflected in wide smiles and verbal enthusiasm, barely hiding the secret of our naughtiness. The anticipation is worth the wait as we rush home to try out our new apparel and play out our erotic roles.

OCTOBER 15

Showing Love

Love is more than sex.

You touch me, caress me, and kiss me—without demands for sex. You allow me to feel close and safe with you. I trust you completely. Other times we may mistakenly think that kissing and drawing the other's body close to us, is a signal for sex. **Today we directly communicate and agree with each other that these "preludes" are a means of expressing love on a daily basis.** We can freely express both verbal and physical affection, knowing that these demonstrations of love do not have to be followed by sexual intimacy. Thank you for loving me so completely.

OCTOBER 16

Living Fully

We go through life only once which is why I am so passionate with you.

Time is too valuable for staying angry or being aloof and removed from you. I want to be totally present with you… to fullty express, in my own words and deeds, how much I love you and appreciate all you do for me and for our family. Did I take the time to hug you when you came into the room, or to look up and listen as you spoke? **Today I acknowledge your presence with my eyes, words, and gestures.**

OCTOBER 17

Holding Hands

I hold your hand in mine and trace the lifelines in your palms.

Today I hold and kiss your hand. I study your hand and commit it to memory as I touch your fingers… your joints… and finally, your knuckles. I examine and stroke the creases and calluses that hint of the life you've lived. I trace your lifelines, cherishing their definition. Everything about you is extraordinary and precious to me.

OCTOBER 18

Sharing Quality Time

Time together can be exhilarating, fun, and provide a window to our souls.

We sometimes waste time talking about mundane topics. Time with you is cherished, as is the quality of the interactions with you that differentiates our relationship from all others. We talk and become so engrossed in each other's words that we can lose our sense of time, distance, and even direction while driving. All of a sudden, we notice we've driven past the exit that we were so intent on finding. Or perhaps, we reached our destination much too quickly. Thank heaven we have the drive back to continue our magical time together! **Today we focus on the quality of our conversations and our interactions to heighten the enjoyment of our time together.**

OCTOBER 19

Recapturing Our Playfulness

We interrupt our routines and become childlike again.

As children, we loved to jump on big piles of dried, crunchy fallen leaves—excitedly disrupting the freshly raked stacks and filling the air with our raucous laughter and enthusiasm. As we became adults, we became more focused on the raking, the gathering of leaves and disposing of them neatly and efficiently. **Just for today we rejoice in the autumn ritual by jumping into the leafy piles, uninhibited in time and place, and paving the way for a fresh approach to revitalize our relationship.**

OCTOBER 20

Being Ourselves

> I cannot completely do things the way you would want me to, and I admit you cannot either.

Neither of us holds a crystal ball in which to see exactly what the other wants us to do and say. However, I pledge to be open about my needs and wants so that you do not have to guess about them. I commit to do my best to let go of specific expectations of how I feel you should be. **Today we agree to avoid making assumptions of what either of us wants or needs. Instead we agree to directly ask what the other is thinking, feeling, or wanting... opening the way to true intimacy.**

OCTOBER 21

Making Out

> Passionately hugging and kissing, is definitely the most fun we've had without laughing.

When we were dating, we'd eagerly wait for the time when we could "make out." During those times of being together, we eagerly hugged and kissed as if we were devouring the other after a rather prolonged fast. Sometimes, we couldn't wait long enough to be alone, distracting a bartender, or another person who may have viewed our unbridled passion. **Tonight we drive to a secluded scenic spot, pretending to be teenagers, and again enjoy those passionate encounters.**

OCTOBER 22

Wanting The Best For Our Partner

True love is about wanting what is best for you.

Sometimes we feel conflicted because we want the other to do something we want, not what is necessarily the best choice for them. And, even though the consequence may not be what I desire, I help you achieve that which will benefit you the most. When you are happier, you spread joy to our family and me. **Today I encourage and support you to seek your desires by listening to what you want and sincerely offering my assistance.**

OCTOBER 23

Enjoying Nature's Bounty

Autumn is the perfect time to take a trip to the mountains.

Autumn reminds us how our world is metamorphosing from many shades of green to various hues of yellow, gold, orange, and red. We take a trip to the mountains or a park to enjoy the changing of color and the beauty surrounding us. Nature patiently waits for us, revealing its stunning splendor and drama when we take time to see it. We soak in its tranquility, refreshing ourselves for the work week ahead. **Today we hold hands and sit in quiet meditation alone with nature.**

OCTOBER 24

Listening To Our Child

At times, listening reveals the best information.

As parents, we tediously endured many thankless carpool trips, as we transported crowds of, rowdy classmates and groups of happy, unrestrained children We might feel insignificant and invisible; yet, these moments can be the best times—if we just listen. The lively chatter emanating from the young passengers in the back seat provides clues to their happiness, well-being, sense of esteem, and warns of any potential problems. **Today and every day when the final rider is dropped off, I listen intently to what our child has to say. Listening in the car can be the best of times.**

OCTOBER 25

Counting Blessings

Lying close to you, I count my blessings.

So many nights when I lay close to you, I lovingly watch you as you sleep, gently touching you, all the while, counting my blessings and scarcely believing that I found you… that we are together. Even after all these years, you seem too good to be real! **Tonight I come to bed, intentionally remaining awake until you drift off to sleep.** In this way I can fully take in your restful sleep and study everything about you, while I thank the heavens for their gift to me.

OCTOBER 26

Sharing Reminders

We can remind each other in helpful ways.

You intuitively sense when I am busy or harried. You assist in making my life smoother by giving me reminders from time to time of items and events that I may forget. Sometimes you leave me written messages or call to meet before a forthcoming obligation. I appreciate these reminders as they help me navigate my day and to keep you close. **Today we discuss the types of reminders that can be helpful to us.**

OCTOBER 27

Non-Verbal Messages

Today we talk with our eyes.

At times we lose our close ties to each other, being too caught up in our demanding, multi-faceted lives. **Today, we express our thoughts and emotions with our eyes.** Remember that look we noticed from across the room, those meaningful glances that suggested we were interested in the other? Or, as our relationship progressed, the look that said I adore you and "only have eyes for you." Today let's see if we still have that touch. Can I send you messages with my eyes?

OCTOBER 28

Sharing New Information

As I learn new skills to promote communication, I share them with you.

Whatever we learn, we often teach it to each other. When I learn new skills, such as those which might develop better communication or could help us more productively direct our emotions and energies, I am so eager to tell you about them. When I return from a workshop or am introduced to a new idea, you are the one to whom I excitedly reveal my new information or skill. Everyday sources of new information on the Internet or television are also conveyed. Thus, as we gain more knowledge and as our relationship continues to become stronger, we find we are the best teachers for each other. **Together we commit to sharing new information and skills to strengthen our union.**

OCTOBER 29

Exploring

Sometimes it's fun to be like a monkey, intently focused on your every feature, while I tirelessly groom you.

I tease your whiskers, running my flattened fingers back and forth on your stubbles, feeling your skin underneath. I gently touch your lips, outlining them with my fingertips and kissing them before I generously apply a moistening ointment, softening your seductive lips even more. I tenderly stroke your eyebrows before gently touching the softness of your feathery lashes. **Today I lavish you with touch and enjoy every moment as I explore your face.**

OCTOBER 30

Experimenting With Sexual Delights

Variety enlivens our lovemaking.

Over time, the excitement of sexual foreplay and intercourse can become mundane, and predictable routines can grow to be boring over the course of time. This sameness ultimately leads to an avoidance of sexual intimacy. We allow ourselves to experiment with different ways to stimulate each other, taking clues from books. We remain open to trying different positions and engaging in foreplay and intercourse in different settings. Perhaps we make love in the kitchen, in the living room by the fire, by the pool, or even in the seclusion of a romantic tent. **Today we open ourselves to experimenting in different ways as we demonstrate our love and passion.**

OCTOBER 31

Celebrating Halloween

We disguise ourselves in the cleverest ways to create a visual "treat" for each other.

Halloween has become one of our favorite occasions. We find it ripe with memories of our child's early costumes and unbridled joy as she excitedly ran from house to house collecting candy and compliments. It's also a time for us to reminisce and laugh about the costumes that we donned as children. **Today we enjoy the holiday's fun by creating and trying on costumes as we join in our child's excitement of playful disguises.**

176

november

Words

The power of our words lies in our intention.

Ironically, especially during difficult times throughout my life, thinking and writing my thoughts, feelings, affirmations and gratitude helped me stay in balance, lessen stress, and avoid being overwhelmed by circumstances. Positive changes in my mind, body, and spirit emerged when I would think of people, events, and the love in my life. Now at mealtimes or quiet times together as a couple or as a family, we tell each other what we are grateful for. We each speedily take turns recounting our blessings, whether big or small, and playing off each other's gratitude. **Today and everyday, we say three things we are grateful for at the beginning of a meal.** By starting conversations with gratitude, we notice our conversations and energies are immediately uplifted, setting the tone for happier and smoother conversations. By focusing on abundance, opportunities, and blessings in our daily lives, we immediately send our energies and spirits higher—for ourselves and those around us.

NOVEMBER 2

Awakening In Your Arms

I awaken to you holding me in your arms.

What a perfect way to start the day! So many mornings before I open my eyes, I become aware of your body touching mine, your arms wrapping around my body, and pulling me even closer. These are the times when I become as one with you, so close that I can feel and hear your breath, the movement of your chest and stomach, and the beating of your heart. Our union is complete. **Today before I get out of bed, I cuddle next to you to feel your presence and to show you how much I care.**

NOVEMBER 3

Sexual Playfulness

Sex can be surprising.

Our splurging and experiencing sexual intimacy for the first time on satin sheets was quite a treat. We oh, so eagerly laid our bodies between the sheets, indulging in the feel of such cool, sensuous fibers. As our bodies began to gravitate towards each other, and we initiated the rhythms of life, we found ourselves slipping on those outrageous red sheets. We laughed hysterically as our act of love turned into a comedic adventure and became a priceless moment. **Today we introduce a playful element into our love making to create unforgettable memories and endearing moments with each other.**

NOVEMBER 4

Words

The power of our words lies in our intention.

As we mature as individuals, we are less prone to simply react. Instead we choose our words more carefully. We understand words can wound us in ways that leave scars. We delight in the belief that words can be healing, with the power to stimulate growth in our relationship, as well as to calm and reassure us. **Today we recognize and commit to looking at our motives or intentions before we simply respond.** We allow ourselves to love consciously and mindfully.

NOVEMBER 5

Writing Poetry

Love poems are a tribute of my affection for you.

Poetry can be magical in its simplicity. It can also be complex and fluid, its rhythmic cadence easily matching the words and sounds. When you have taken the time to write love poems to me, they are forever prized. I realize the extra effort you have taken to create them for me—these poems truly personalize your words of love. **Today, I write a poem to you to show you how much you mean to me to signify you are most cherished.**

NOVEMBER 6

Relaxing Together

When I want to relax, I visualize your smile and feel your touch.

Taking a brief respite, we close our eyes and picture us being in a serene, exotic location, perhaps in mountains or near aquamarine waters. Here we are able to feel tranquil and restful. My favorite way to relax is imagining your smile and feeling your hands soothing my muscles and spirit. Through my imagination, my mind cannot distinguish reality from fantasy. Almost instantly, I feel your presence by my side. I glow and purr… content and peaceful in the aura of your compassion and touch. **Today we each visualize a tranquil environment, capturing the sights, sounds, colors, intensity, sensations, smells, and taste as we imagine being transported to a place of comfort.**

NOVEMBER 7

Being Aware

I must first become aware before I can understand and change my behaviors.

Sometimes I'm on some kind of auto-pilot… repeatedly practicing self-sabotaging behaviors and reactions. When I respond with fear, sadness, or anger, I look inward to determine what I am saying or thinking that propels my distress. I take time to decode my self-talk, so I can change the way I respond to events. By choosing the way I view situations, I can then better choose my responses rather than letting my emotions drive me. **Today I take time to examine my thoughts before I respond, knowing it allows me to empower myself to be healthier and fully present in the moment.**

NOVEMBER 8

Rhythms Of The Ocean

As ocean waves roll back and forth, they symbolize the give and take, and the harmony of our love.

Life began in the ocean. We delight in seeing the ocean— sometimes it is calm, much like our relationship; other times it is as turbulent and furious as our anger. The water is cleansing, supporting life in varied forms, or it can sting as the salt penetrates our wounds. Just as in our marriage, the sea serves as a reminder that we can rhythmically flow toward the other through teamwork and sharing, or we can be antagonistic with ferocious energy. **Today we recommit to talking and sharing until we restore our relationship to the tranquility of quiet waters.**

NOVEMBER 9

Parenting

Our unity survives the challenges of raising children.

Our child has tried to outsmart us to get her own way, whether that means going to the mall, movies with her friends, or enjoying a sleep over. Through consistent communication with each other, we establish ground rules to guide us in determining a unified course of action. If we work together, she has less of a chance of pitting us against the other. "Go ask your mother" or "go ask your father" are not options in our household. Rather, she must present the request to both of us. **Today we are united in our parenting to keep our marriage strong.** Only then can we survive the rigors of parenthood.

NOVEMBER 10

Creating The Mood

We have all the resources to create the moods we desire.

We are seldom satisfied for events to just "happen" to us. Instead, we decide consciously to choose the course of our day and how our actions improve our relationship. We cook together to enjoy a tantalizing meal at home with candlelight and soft music. Sometimes we sit on the patio to gaze at a sunset while we eat our meals, observing the changing hues of the landscape and the birds quickly returning to their nests as darkness nears. Other times we retreat to the quiet of our bathroom, lightly scenting the air and water with bath gels and oils to provide relaxing aromatherapy that reduces our stress and calms us. **Today we empower ourselves by creating the ambiance we desire to enhance our relationship.**

NOVEMBER 11

Touching

We nourish our skin, the largest organ in our body.

Whenever we take a hot shower together, or one immediately follows the other, we lovingly apply lotion on the other's back. We all need to be touched, our skin naturally craving this nurturing touch on a daily basis. Touch takes on many forms whether it is smoothing your hair, scratching your back, massaging your foot, or lightly imparting butterfly kisses to your checks. **Each day we make a conscious effort to include a variety of touches to nourish our bodies and our souls.**

NOVEMBER 12

Affirming Of Our Love

Each day we say to each other in words and action we are so happy to be together.

Daily, I hear the words, "I'm so happy to be married to you. You are so perfect for me." Radiating from your comments, I feel grateful and loving toward you. I then reciprocate warmly in a natural and easy way. We smile, squeeze each other's hand, hug, kiss, and still have that twinkle in our eyes. We draw closer to each other whenever we hear these proclamations. Always fresh, the more loving affirmations are said through the years, the more we feel as if our love is magical. **Today we tell each other, "You are perfect for me."**

NOVEMBER 13

Sharing Family Time

Enriching our family time stimulates our love as partners and encourages bonding as a family.

We eat, play, and work together around the home. One of our cherished nightly activities is reading together. From the beginning, when our child was an infant—unable to understand the full context of the exact words—but fully able to comprehend the intent and meanings expressed… we read to her. As she grew older, we incorporated reading into a bedtime ritual. We all snuggled into bed together and read or listened to stories. **Tonight, no matter the age of our child, we crawl into bed together and enjoy story time.**

NOVEMBER 14

Being Polite

We treat each other as best friends, showing respect, kindness, and appreciation.

One hallmark of our relationship is the display of politeness and consideration for each other. We often inquire about the other's wants. We are careful to include courteous expressions: "please" and "thank you" in our daily lives. It's almost as if we are polite strangers, practicing etiquette, but with the comfort and ease of best friends who seem to sense the other's needs, desires, and moods—creating the best balance of all. **Today we display politeness and our best manners with each other to show our respect, appreciation, and love.**

NOVEMBER 15

Shopping Together

When you and I go shopping, you give me your opinions in a loving way.

I love to "shop till I drop!" You are not quite as passionate or exhilarated by shopping sprees as I am, yet you indulge me by going to the malls, and sitting patiently while I paw through a myriad of garments and model a few of the outfits for you. You are patient and fully engaged, even when I know you are only along to keep me company. Ordinary, yet uncommon gestures like this show how much you love me. **Today I return your loving gesture by doing an activity of your choice.**

NOVEMBER 16

Understanding Silence

Silence can be peaceful and healing, or it can be a sign that our relationship is hurting.

We crave silence at times. It is critical to have the wonderful gift of solitude to replenish our minds, bodies, and spirit. Unfortunately, silence can also indicate our relationship is in trouble. Maybe we are angry with each other and "giving the silent treatment" as punishment. It can also be the unfortunate sign that we are starting to distance ourselves from each other, having less in common. I heed the signs of silence and use this as an opportunity to communicate with you if I detect we may be detaching. **I want our relationship to be vibrant forever with love and sharing.**

NOVEMBER 17

Giving

As Thanksgiving approaches, I clean my closet to share with those in need.

We have so much abundance in each other's love as well as being rich with material possessions. **Today I tackle purging the clutter in my closet in order to honestly confront those items taking up valuable space, and remaining unused season after season.** As I inspect each item, determining whether to keep or discard, I am mindful of how I could help others by donating my unused items. Through giving, I am even more thankful for all we have.

NOVEMBER 18

Letting Go

When I attempt to control you, I know that something is out of balance.

Sometimes it is so difficult to let go of controlling you. I am determined to convince and motivate you to do what I think or want you to do. Today I choose to let go of controlling a simple behavior such as wearing shoes in the house or pressing you to change the way you load the plates and glasses into the dishwasher. At times when I'm physically and emotionally tired, I realize I'm trying to change you. Because you determine your own course of action, you have the final say, and you are in charge of your own thoughts and feelings. **Today I remind myself to let go as I can only control myself. By letting go, I show my love and respect for you.**

NOVEMBER 19

Initiating Sexuality

I desire you and initiate a loving sexual contact with you.

Passionate flames still burn, and when they do, I initiate sexual intimacy with you. By doing so, I am communicating to you in a direct physical manner that I love you and long for your body and your touch. I don't have to play games and wait for you to make the first sexual gesture. **Today I show my fond affection by demonstrating my sexual love for you.**

NOVEMBER 20

Sharing Work

I take my partner to work today.

To describe our day at work is not quite the same as experiencing it. To appreciate what we each do in our work environment, we need to experience it directly. We've taken our sons, daughters, and pets, to work but rarely our mate. By taking you to work, I am showing you how proud I am of the job I do, and how proud I am to introduce you to my colleagues. Similarly, I hunger to know more about your career challenges and what excites you about your endeavors. Coming home at night, after spending the majority of our waking hours at work, we are better able to understand and empathize with each other. **Today I emotionally support you in every way by better understanding the reality of your work day and the people around you.**

NOVEMBER 21

Giving Thanks

Our heads are bowed and our eyes are closed in earnest and heartfelt prayer for God's guidance for our family, love, health, and all the blessings of friends, jobs, and school.

Thanksgiving is not a once a year event. It is the daily gratitude felt in our hearts, cherishing all the blessings that we have in our lives. We have so much to be thankful for. Each day brings us so many gifts of supportive and caring family, friends, joy, beauty, lifestyle, anticipation, peace, and above all, love. **Today, and every day, we happily commit to graciously giving thanks for the blessings and miracles in our daily lives and for His sharing these incredible gifts.**

NOVEMBER 22

Willingness To Help

If you're beating me badly at a game, you offer advice on how I can capitalize on my misfortunes.

We help each other whether winning or losing. Whenever either one of us experiences difficulties in a game, skill, or task, we stop and assist. We examine problems and offer constructive advice, sometimes to our undoing if the match is close. We play fair in the most important game of life. **Today we embrace that we are partners for life, there to assist and enrich the other rather than considering the other as a competitor.**

NOVEMBER 23

Crying Tears Of Joy

Our union is complete when both of us are free to cry.

At times I may cry when I experience "beautiful moments." As we have gradually grown closer spiritually and emotionally, as well as physically, I've noticed that you also have tears in your eyes. These tears can be prompted by music that reminds us of the birth of our daughter or reading words that attest to our love. Crying is truly the deepest intimacy that we experience as a couple; feeling free to express and release all emotions. **Today we discuss a moment when we've cried, confirming to the other that these tears are truly healing.**

NOVEMBER 24

Cravings

When we have cravings we look inside ourselves for clues.

When we feel that undeniable urge to eat chocolates, drink alcohol, or go shopping, we freeze and study our internal needs. Are we really hungry or are we simply feeling tired, sad, anxious, stressed, lonely, bored or frustrated? Do we tell ourselves that it's okay to eat several pieces of cake, because we've had such a tough day? Is the cake what we earnestly want, or is it simply to comfort and pacify us? When we discover the true meanings behind our cravings, we learn to love ourselves more. **Today we examine our thoughts and feelings that lead to our cravings and compulsions, and find true inner answers to meet our needs.**

NOVEMBER 25

Calling On My Helper

My faith and belief in my "helper" sustain me through difficult times.

We each have within us an ideal helper, guide, mentor, God, or a spirit that is present with us during times of struggle. Sometimes you, my beloved, cannot lift my burdens enough. It may be because you are physically unavailable or my fear and despair are so great. During those times, I close my eyes and imagine my special helper coming to me. I visualize all the qualities of my helper and surround myself with its voice, words, and touch. I listen for the encouragement I so desperately need to hear. My helper seems to know exactly what comforts me. I feel a soothing touch comforting me. **Today I thank you, my helper, for always being there in my times of greatest need; knowing I can visualize and dialogue with you any time.**

NOVEMBER 26

Cuddling

As the nights become colder, the more we cuddle.

Cold winds sometimes blow loudly outside, and disturb the solitude of the night and swaying the shrubs and tree limbs. As the temperature drops, we are signaled to bundle and to seek the warmth and comfort of our partner's body. We gravitate towards each other, entwined in the other's embrace, feeling protected and insulated from the harshness. **Today we take time to snuggle together, feeling at once warmer and blanketed in each other's love.**

NOVEMBER 27

Trusting Inner Feelings

I am secure in trusting my inner feelings

It is understood that sometimes you and I hold different feelings and points of view. You may want me to choose an action that somehow doesn't feel quite right to me. You are confident in doing things that are right for you—your recommendation, however, may not be the right path for me to follow. During those times when your solutions may not seem to fit me, I embrace listening to my feelings and trusting them to help guide me to my own level of enlightenment. **I am secure and safe in our relationship, knowing I am not bound to follow your suggestions to placate you or to minimize conflict.** After all, this is exactly why you love me, and I love you for being honest and following your own feelings.

NOVEMBER 28

Having Fun

I lovingly kiss and lick the crumbs from your face.

You remain the ultimate master at keeping me smiling and laughing… and amusing me with your ready, quick wit and clever antics. Today, when I inform you that you have some food on the corner of your lips, you quickly respond with, "Will you kiss it off?" **These impromptu retorts reduce me to happy tears at times when we are being silly and obviously enjoying each other's company so much. I am thrilled to be with you!**

NOVEMBER 29

Strengthening Our Connection

When I openly recognize and show appreciation for your daily contributions, your self esteem and our bonding together as a couple soar.

When we encourage each other, whether through compliments or a simple acknowledgement of the other's actions, we also increase the chances of that behavior reoccurring. **I notice certain changes in you, and now consciously commit to showing you my increased appreciation and recognition of your efforts**. Without recognition and acknowledgement, a number of golden opportunities would be missed in which I could create feel good situations on a daily basis for you to be loved, appreciated, and feel even closer to me. I am now viewing you with love rather than criticism, paving the way for our love to grow even more.

NOVEMBER 30

Parenting

As I see you interact with our child, I feel closer and more loving towards you.

You are an incredible parent... holding, kissing, hugging, talking, teaching, guiding, disciplining, and playing with our child. These nurturing behaviors come so naturally to you. You had the best times playing games and doing artistic crafts with our child early Saturday mornings while you let me sleep in. The "two can do" projects became prized collectables for us. Other times while traveling, you would share playful correspondence by sending detailed messages back and forth between imaginary characters. You would quickly scribble notes to these delightful characters, with accompanying drawings. These dialogues were absolutely creative, funny, and oh, so playful. Thank you for being such a wonderful parent. We are so truly blessed. **Today we engage in a creative, light hearted dialogue, craft, or game with our child**.

december

DECEMBER 1

Purpose

Our love is for sharing with others.

Do you ever ponder your purpose in life? I am inclined to think our greatest gift to ourselves and others is to give and receive love. By generously giving love, we receive it back in so many ways. We make another's day so much brighter with love… providing hope, energy, and happiness. **I resolve to share my love with you, our child, and whomever we may encounter**. By showing affection and affirming others, we become teachers and healers in everyday life, positively impacting all whom we meet.

DECEMBER 2

Healthy Choices

I use your love to assist me in practicing healthy behaviors.

As the holidays near, we are called upon to respond to the vast array of tantalizing foods which follows us everywhere. I am faced with far too many temptations to eat, drink, and to overindulge. I remind myself I can eat when I'm hungry and thoroughly enjoy whatever I consume. I know I can choose to stop when I am full. Knowing there are many days of food and beverage ahead to entice me with flavorful textures, aromas, and remembrances of their tastiness, I consume smaller amounts. I do not allow food or drinks to act as substitutes for my need for love. **Today I choose to drink and eat in a healthy manner because I value myself and you.**

DECEMBER 3

Quality Time

We make routine tasks a time of intimacy.

We take our dog for a daily walk. Rather than dreading it as a chore, we consider that daily walk as an opportunity to gain some outdoor exercise and quality time to talk. The conversation is long on the revelations of our day, making our walk too short. We share our responses to the day's events. Because of these walks, we become aware of important thoughts, feelings, and events. **Today we turn a commonplace task into a time of quality in sharing our love.**

DECEMBER 4

Displaying Photographs

I lovingly choose a photograph of you to display at work.

When we are truly in love, we want the entire world to know about our loved one,. We are unable to say enough about the other, and find numerous reasons for complimenting their virtues. We also want to "show off" pictures of our mate and family. Photographs of our loved ones fill our working space with vibrations of lightness and warmth. These pictures remind us of memorable moments and gestures; helping us to stay connected even when we are apart. **Today I proudly and loving choose and display a photograph of you to keep you close to my heart.**

DECEMBER 5

Using Our Brains

God gave us two sides of the brain... to work together.

The right brain is often the artistic and emotional side while the left brain is the logical, analytical decoder. We often stop to admire the wonderful marriage... even of our brains. How beautifully our exquisite minds provide a glorious mix of spontaneous feelings and creativity which integrate processing of rational thought by using skills from both sides of our brain. Sometimes, we allow one side of our brains to control and dominate, ignoring and being unaware of the other valuable pieces of information when we make decisions. **Today and every day, we use all of our brain's capacity to help guide us in resolving conflicts, making productive decisions, and elevating our love to even greater heights of romance, passion, and intimacy.**

DECEMBER 6

Sharing Christmas Activities

Our holidays are merrier when we experience decorating as a family.

As children we loved the Christmas holidays. We'd pass through rows of trees to find the perfectly shaped one for our home. We excitedly set up the tree and began to decorate with prized handmade ornaments and miles of tiny lights. Anticipating Santa's big day, we conjured up our gift list. The holidays can be the best time for us to be with our family. **We choose to share the magic of Christmas dreams coming true with those we love.**

DECEMBER 7

Learning From The Past

All of my experiences in life have prepared me for who I am today.

Sometimes I am filled with sorrow for certain losses and difficulties emanating from my past. However, these painful experiences clearly serve to provide me strength so I can overcome my emotional wounds. When healing takes place, I can more easily evolve into a happier and healthier being. By acknowledging my losses from the past, I allow myself time to grieve. Then, like the earth reawakening, my spirits and skills become stronger. I then learn to accept myself even more. No longer bound by feelings of inadequacy and inferiority, I can discard my shame. My influence affects you as I become wiser and healthier, because as I overcome psychological pain, I gain new insights, and skills, and change my ways of responding. **By working through my adversities, I am now capable of more fully loving myself and you.**

DECEMBER 8

Enhancing Our Sexuality

As we age, our sexual connectedness remains.

When we were children, it seemed unfathomable for us to imagine our parents were having sex. Now that we are living longer, we may still think that our grandparents' sexual intimacy disappeared many years ago. Desire for our partners does not have to diminish with age. We do not have to lose our sexual functioning. **As we age and become intimate with each other, we become creative in the ways we show love, exploring even more ways to stimulate and arouse the senses during intimacy.** Sex does not necessarily mean intercourse—it is an extension of ourselves—and enjoyed in the most private and intimate ways.

DECEMBER 9

Exercising Together

When we exercise together, we help each other reach our goals.

I love exercising with you. We may be swimming laps where I do my best to match your tempo and the intensity of your strokes. When we work out with weights in the gym, I am encouraged as you guide me on how to work each piece of equipment. You might demonstrate your lifting routine. **Guiding me as a personal trainer, you instruct and motivate me to press or pull harder. You show your love by assisting me to have a stronger and healthier body.**

DECEMBER 10

Jumping Into Your Arms

I run to you, jump into your arms, and wrap my arms and legs around you.

This eruption of our love was witnessed by our beloved child when we modeled unbridled, affection for each other. Within our home, expressions of love are diverse and we openly celebrate when a family member comes home from work, school, or an errand. We laugh and give a group hug and kiss. You have even remarked this is the reason you continue to exercise and work out as you carried me around the room. Our child, too, enjoyed jumping into your arms as if she were a member of the circus. **Today we rejoice in our love and our embrace.**

DECEMBER 11

Celebrating Our First Meeting

We celebrate the moment we met.

How could two people in this vast universe come together at exactly the precise time to meet, connect, and initiate conversations? **Today we discuss how we first met and experience again the flood of excited and happy emotions**. We felt energized, alive, elated, curious, and eager to get to know each other. Time stood still when we met. We were lost—soaking in all the marvelous qualities of each other. The smiles, the sparkle and friendly eyes,... each drew our attention to every verbal and nonverbal detail. I was swept off my feet by your humor, wit, and charm. A magnet seemed to hold us spellbound, as we both eagerly waited to learn more about this fascinating, unbelievable person.

DECEMBER 12

Staying Young

Listening to our child's music keeps us young.

Listening to the tunes our child has downloaded onto her digital player, while at home or in the car, leads to both quiet smiling and amusement. Some are hilarious parodies, bad singing describes several, others have a great beat or rapping messages, and a few are downright "trashy." Yet, they all provide us with a glimpse of our child's habits and interests. Above all, these songs are a springboard for laughter and discussion, bonding us as a family. "Hey, we're cool!" **Today we both remain open and listen to music of another generation.**

DECEMBER 13

Forgiving Myself

By forgiving myself, I can forgive you.

In order to love you fully, I realize that it is important to forgive myself. When I am generous and tender towards myself, I learn that I can better demonstrate these behaviors towards you when I felt injured by your comment or action. When I write a loving letter to myself, as if I were writing to a best friend… or as a loving adult to a hurting child, I affirm that mistakes and misdeeds do not define me. Instead, these mistakes and regrettable acts allow me to go to a deeper level of love and forgiveness of self. These errors also give me valuable information as to how I want to live my life and future choices that I might make. **Today, I write a loving letter to myself to release my burden of guilt and shame so I may feel peaceful and worthy.**

DECEMBER 14

Remembering Those We Love

The holidays are a time to pause and remember those we love.

As the holidays draw near, we are truly grateful for our family and close friends. **Today we take the time to call and write our friends and family members to let them know how much we value their friendship and support.** When we take time to exchange warm messages and to catch up with each other's lives, we cement our bond. By making time for those we cherish, our relationships are renewed and our affection is reciprocated.

DECEMBER 15

Caroling

Singing makes us feel free and liberated.

Singing from our hearts frees us from the accumulating stress brought on by the burden of our responsibilities. It's especially fun to harmonize with people. We are totally uninhibited, throwing caution to the wind, and freely sing in the shower, whether perfectly or completely off key. Nothing matters but having this lighthearted moment with you as we smile, chuckle, and laugh at our exaggerated voices. **Today we go door-to-door caroling with friends and family to share some fun and sense of community.**

DECEMBER 16

Physical Connections

I long for your touch.

I love the way you voluntarily rub my back when we stand in line at the grocery store and movies, or when I'm cooking dinner at home. You indulge me with your acts of kindness when I least expect them. I know that you treasure me just being with you. **Today I surprise you with loving touch in the areas of your body that you crave.**

DECEMBER 17

Picking Our Battles

We assess the intensity and depth of our needs and wants.

We dislike the terms "win or lose," due to the connotation that one of us will be unhappy. Sometimes we seem to be at a deadlock when we disagree on a mutual decision and action. When we seem to be at a stalemate, we can choose to avoid a power struggle from occurring. After discussing the importance of this decision, we ask each other to rate how strong that need or want is at that time on a scale of zero to one hundred. To be fair, we look inward for what this decision means to us and be honest about the importance of "getting our way." Whichever one of us has the higher number is honored with having the final decision. When we are sincere in wanting the best for the other, our love emerges and we willingly yield to the other's desire in a gracious and affectionate way. The chances are likely, the next time, the gracious one will be the recipient of the loving decision. **Today we honestly ask ourselves to rate an outcome that we both desire, and help the one with the higher rating to achieve that goal.**

DECEMBER 18

Planning Activities Together

You choose an activity for us to enjoy.

Resentment can occasionally surface when one of us gets our way more often than the other. To keep our relationship fresh and balanced, we take turns planning activities, ensuring that each of us is content with our leisure pastimes. We initiate discussions of prospective events, often choosing together what we'd like to do! **Today is your day to describe an activity you would enjoy pursuing. I can hardly wait.**

DECEMBER 19

Accepting Our Differences

Holidays teach us about love and acceptance.

During the holiday season, as we approach acquaintances and strangers, we greet them with "happy holidays!" We are becoming aware of different cultures and traditions, no longer presuming our way is the correct standard. We include our relationship in that widening circle of love and acceptance, talking directly about differences and preferences—preventing us from mind reading and guessing what the other would want. **As a couple we enthusiastically endorse our differences, which in turn magnifies greater acceptance for our uniqueness.**

DECEMBER 20

Toasting

Socially we toast friends and occasions. Now we toast our love.

We include our love and relationship in a toast at social gatherings. After all, there is no better way to celebrate than with a fresh acknowledgement of our love. Every meal or every drink can be an opportunity for a celebration of living life with each other, fully enraptured with the present. **Today we celebrate and embrace our love growing fuller with every passing day.**

DECEMBER 21

Winter

The cold stillness of winter allows us to restore our body, mind, and spirit.

Winter is known as time of hibernation for some animals. Likewise, this also can be a time for us to be still... in contemplation, reclaiming our energies, and also healing our bodies. We use this day to allow our bodies to rest and recover from our speedy, productive pace. We are able to enjoy resting and sleeping in without guilt or undue pressure to achieve. **Through leisure, we are able to bloom with a renewed clarity of what is important to us and to our relationship.**

DECEMBER 22

Giving Notes Of Love

You flood me with written messages of love and admiration.

We frequently give each other multiple greeting cards, because we love each other—we often give more cards than we do gifts to express our sentiment. These kind and loving actions further spread joy in our home. Sometimes there are two or three cards expressing our love and gratitude that are left for the other to find throughout the day. We are so blessed to have each other in our lives and these cards mean more than any of the gifts received on special occasions. These loving cards are kept forever. **Today I give you multiple cards and notes of love to convey my love and appreciation.**

DECEMBER 23

Enjoying Holiday Lights

Holiday light displays transport us to a magical world.

The merriment our child shows as she watches the animated reindeers and twinkling lights is sheer wonderment. We share in her innocence and purity of childhood as we see the world through her eyes. It's as if we are riveted by our first experience of the breath-taking beauty, drama, and fantasy this holiday brings. **Today we visit holiday light displays and view them through childlike wonderment.**

DECEMBER 24

Worshiping

Candlelight services remind us of the real reason we celebrate Christmas.

Every Christmas Eve when we attend church, my eyes well with tears as we joyfully sing holiday carols, depicting the wonder of our Savior's birth. These lyrics remind me of the true, deep meaning of Christmas and the many blessings in our lives. My gratitude and love for you is embedded deep in my heart. This is also a time when we are reminded of the hardships that so many children and their families have to bear. **Today we sincerely wish and pray for all the people of the world to feel the blessings of Christmas with messages of hope, peace, and the miracle of life.**

DECEMBER 25

Santa

I smile every time I think of you as Santa.

You stuffed a pillow in your belly and donned a Santa outfit, and… without my assistance, you proudly painted perfect round circles for your rosy red cheeks. I laughed out loud when I saw you, and our child stared at you in wonder. Her curious gaze suggested you somehow looked and sounded vaguely familiar. "That Santa with the daddy-face," was the way she described you. You presented her with Santa's gifts and away you flew, leaving behind a lifetime of memories for our daughter and me. **Today I wish Merry Christmas to all and for love to be everywhere!**

DECEMBER 26

Sharing Magical Holidays

We are suspended in childlike delight as we talk about our most memorable holidays.

Holidays help us to see the world through a child's eyes full of wonder, excitement, and awe. They squeal with exhuberant aliveness and euphoria while opening their presents. Even little gifts can elicit such enormous delight and a cacophony of laughter from pure happiness. Vicariously, we feel their pleasure while watching them. For a short time, we are children too, caught up in their excitement—shared smiles, joyful roars, and bursts of energy. We feel the closeness of our family. We joyously share the essence of the holiday magic of surprise, giggles, and immeasurable happiness. **Today we discuss our fondest memories of holidays and gifts that we have received.**

DECEMBER 27

Growing Closer Together

Our relationship becomes better with time.

Like wine, our love grows better with time. We can be ourselves, no longer having to impress the other... we have become more confident and secure. Our increased positive self esteem helps us to accept each other more easily. We have learned skills to negotiate our differences so we can resolve conflicts rather than playing the role of peacemaker for the sake of making our relationship smoother. Most of all, our passion and zest for each other continue to grow as we discover even more reasons to appreciate and love one another. **Today I still want to shout from the mountaintops, "I love you!"**

DECEMBER 28

Cherish Time Together

When the weekend is over, we take the time to remember the highlights of our time together.

Today as you boarded a plane for your trip, you sent me an incredible text message. You thanked me for a wonderful weekend together, entitled "let me count the ways!" You then began to list and describe all the activities that were memorable for you. Before your message, I had considered the weekend to be rather ordinary. Upon reading your message, I was immediately uplifted and realized just how meaningful our times together are for you. I treat each time together with care and enjoy the fulfillment our sharing brings to us.

DECEMBER 29

Gazing Into The Future

We are reborn – our love is just the beginning. The best is yet to come.

We have almost completed one year's journey of examining our relationship. We have looked at ourselves constructively in order to enrich our love for each other, discovering new ways to show our exquisite love and dedication to each other. Together, we have learned and incorporated new actions that positively impacted our relationship and encouraged it to flourish even more. We gratefully acknowledge that we are even more aware of the infinite ways to express love to ourselves and to each other. **Indeed, the best is yet to come as we continue to grow in knowledge, skills, awareness, and closeness.**

DECEMBER 30

Growing Old Together

I want to grow old with you.

You are the one I adore. You are the one that I repeatedly fall in love with daily. You are my confidant, my sage and trusted adviser, my best friend, my lover, my partner, and the most unbelievable parent. You witnessed my emergence from young adulthood to a self-confident person. Shedding all vestiges of shame, I became like the Phoenix bird. You helped me create an even bolder persona. I reinvented myself into an individual whom I liked and loved. Thank you, sweetheart. **Today I tell you "I love you eternally and want to spend the rest of my life with you."** I express to you how you have helped me become a better person by having you in my life.

Reflections

Counting our blessings, we reflect on the ways our love has emerged this year,

Today we take a loving look at the growth of our relationship. We express our love for each other in multi-faceted ways through physical closeness and support, by giving each other gifts, and by words of love, encouragement, and understanding. Both publicly and privately you have said you were the most fortunate person alive with me in your life. You have helped me with so many tasks both personally and professionally. The numerous thoughtful gestures each day convey how much you love me. Our precious time together this year has flown by. We had so much fun and shared so many intimate moments. Thank you for listening to me, and especially for your understanding and acceptance. We have grown healthier and closer together.

Love and kisses forever, my love.

Mamiko

Index

Daily Affirmations for Love

Daily Affirmations for Love

Daily Affirmations for Love

Daily Affirmations for Love

Daily Affirmations for Love

Daily Affirmations for Love

Keeping Passion Alive

Daily Affirmations for Love

Daily Affirmations for Love

Walks	FEBRUARY	20	30
Love Letters	FEBRUARY	22	31
Flowers	FEBRUARY	27	34
Spooning	MARCH	2	38
Kissing	MARCH	7	41
Sleeping Late	MARCH	11	44
Thinking Of You	MARCH	13	46
Public Affection	MARCH	22	51
Pleasuring	MARCH	26	53
Playfully Romantic	MARCH	27	53
Sexiness	APRIL	15	66
Embracing	APRIL	16	67
Sending Flowers	MAY	1	74
Happily In Love	MAY	2	76
Meeting For Lunch	MAY	4	78
Pleasuring Each Other	MAY	6	79
Whispering	MAY	8	80
The Bedroom	MAY	9	80
Create The "Setting"	MAY	13	82
Stroking Your Hair	MAY	16	84
Circle Of Love	JUNE	10	98
Reminiscing	JUNE	12	99
Gifting	JUNE	21	104
Fantasizing	JUNE	23	105
Creating Time Together	JUNE	24	105
Loving Touch	JUNE	30	108

Daily Affirmations for Love

Love is a Verb

Daily Affirmations for Love

Daily Affirmations for Love

Loving Self

Daily Affirmations for Love

Daily Affirmations for Love

Winter	DECEMBER	21	203
Mindful Loving/ Mutual Support			
How Are You?	JANUARY	4	4
Acceptance	JANUARY	8	6
Quality Of Time	JANUARY	12	8
Awareness	JANUARY	17	10
Healing	JANUARY	19	12
Teaching	JANUARY	21	13
Patience	JANUARY	23	14
Tears	JANUARY	28	17
Openness	FEBRUARY	6	22
A Mirror To My Soul	FEBRUARY	8	23
Calm	FEBRUARY	9	24
Personal Best	FEBRUARY	10	25
Listening	FEBRUARY	18	29
Anger	FEBRUARY	21	31
Everyday Gestures	FEBRUARY	25	33
Self-Inventory	MARCH	3	39
Requesting Changes In Behavior	MARCH	10	43
Being Myself	MARCH	16	47
Living In The Present	MARCH	21	50
Teamwork	APRIL	2	58
Letting Go (Step 1)	APRIL	5	60
Healing (Step 2)	APRIL	6	61
Reframing	APRIL	9	63
Emotional Support	APRIL	14	66

Daily Affirmations for Love

Daily Affirmations for Love

Daily Affirmations for Love

Daily Affirmations for Love

Shared Relationships

Daily Affirmations for Love

Simple Joys

Daily Affirmations for Love

Daily Affirmations for Love

Daily Affirmations for Love

Daily Affirmations for Love

Dear Reader,

"I hope you have enjoyed this book and that you have experienced a personal transformation of loving yourself and being even closer to the one you love. My wish for you is to experience the magic of "falling in love" and staying just as passionately in love throughout the years. There's no other experience quite like being in love and being loved!"

May you enjoy the gift of love,

Mamiko

CONNECT NOW WITH THE LEADING AUTHORITY ON OVERCOMING SELF-SABOTAGE IN LOVE, RELATIONSHIPS AND HIGH PERFORMANCE

DR. MAMIKO ODEGARD, LEADING THE ACT ON LOVE™ MOVEMENT AND THE DEVELOPER OF THE 1 HEART 1 MIND METHOD, IS NOW OFFERING LIFE CHANGING VIP INTENSIVE RETREATS AND EXCLUSIVE CONCIERGE PROGRAMS

---

http://www.drmamiko.com/

Facebook

https://www.facebook.com/Dr-Mamiko-104973559851930

https://www.facebook.com/ACTOnLove

Email

Success@DrMamiko.com

LinkedIn

www.linkedin.com/pub/dr-mamiko-odegard/4/b65/140

Google+

https://plus.google.com/+Drmamiko/posts

YouTube

http://bit.ly/Mamiko1Vs2KmL

Author's Request for Reviews

If you enjoyed reading *Daily Affirmations for Love* I would appreciate it if you would help others enjoy the book, too.

- ♡ **LEND IT.** This book is lending enabled, so please feel free to share with a friend.

- ♡ **RECOMMEND IT**. Please help other readers find the book by recommending it to readers' groups, discussion boards, Goodreads, etc.

- ♡ **REVIEW IT.** Please tell others why you liked this book by reviewing it on the site where you purchased it, on your favorite book site, or your own blog. Amazon, being probably the largest distributor of books as the online giant bookstore, makes the review process easy... just click here — http://amzn.to/2edZfOM— then click on the hyperlink, Customer Reviews. You will be taken to just the right area to post your own review of what you liked about the book and what you feel other readers might experieence. Oh, and thank you in advance!

- ♡ **EMAIL ME.** I'd love to hear from you.
  Success@DrMamiko.com

NOTES: